LAC International Press
LeadAcrossCultures.com
info@LeadAcrossCultures.com

ISBN-10: 0615969909
ISBN-13: 978-0615969909
Library of Congress Control Number: 2014900031
Printed in the United States of America

Cover Design – Tom Nixon
Interior Layout – Arlene Cohn
Editor – Michael Carr
Author Photographer – Minh Doan

What Other Experts are Saying

"Lan Bercu has written a business gem that should be part of every leader's flight plan. Packed full of real world anecdotes and case studies, *The 36 Ancient Chinese Strategies for Modern Business* challenges you to re-think typical business execution strategies. This book is a must read if you're seeking a serious competitive advantage in today's international business arena."

LT. COL. ROB WALDO WALDMAN
Author of the national bestseller *Never Fly Solo*

"Lan Bercu has written a powerful and richly textured book based on lessons from her work as a respected cross cultural expert and Vietnamese immigrant. The 36 Stratagems are applicable to people in small and large organizations interested in applying innovative approaches that are based on ancient wisdom. Her compelling stories make this a fantastic read."

JENNIFER B. KAHNWEILER, PH.D., CSP
Author of *The Introverted Leader* and *Quiet Influence*

"Lan Bercu's biography reads like a fascinating novel, but what's even more fascinating is her extraordinary grasp of Eastern wisdom applied to modern business' best practices. If you're looking for new business insights, you'll find plenty in her explanations of the Chinese classic 36 Strategies. Highly recommended."

THOMAS HUYNH, Founder of Sonshi

"Offering a time-tested blueprint to business success, *The 36 Ancient Chinese Strategies for Modern Business* is an essential read for anyone wishing to compete in any economy and especially a global one. Lan Bercu's story is compelling. She is a successful and inspiring entrepreneur, speaker, and author who can help you achieve your dreams as well."

GLEN GOULD
Vice President of Newman-Coweta Chamber of Commerce

"I love this book. Lan Bercu provides fresh insights and fascinating illustrations of how Eastern wisdom applies to modern business. An excellent and timely book that will boost your marketing, sales, and business development success. Thinking about buying this book? Stop thinking - DO IT!"

DAVID NEWMAN
Author of *Do It! Marketing: 77 Instant-Action Ideas to Boost Sales, Maximize Profits, and Crush Your Competition*

"Through fascinating stories and practical suggestions, Lan Bercu dissects the ancient body of Chinese wisdom used to win in both war and business, giving you the advantage you need to become a leader in your field. Answer her questions and you will unlock these secrets for yourself!"

DR. MARCIA REYNOLDS, Global Executive Coach
Author of *The Discomfort Zone:
How Leaders Turn Difficult Conversations into Breakthroughs*

"Drawing on thousands of years of wisdom, Lan Bercu helps us stretch our minds to look at business decision-making in a whole new (but very old) way. By using biographical stories and actual case studies, she gives us a new roadmap to business and life success. Every page has ideas and information you can use immediately! "

STEVE COHN, CSP, Director of Learning, Strativity Group
Author of *It's Not Rocket Service*

"In The 36 Ancient Chinese Strategies for Modern Business, Lan Bercu masterfully weaves history, business acumen and a gift for storytelling into a book that belongs on every business-owner's bedside table. Well-written, clear and inspirational, I can't wait to implement these strategies in my own business."

SANDY WEAVER CARMAN, Author of *The Original MBA*

三十六計

THE
36

ANCIENT CHINESE
STRATEGIES
FOR
MODERN BUSINESS

LAN BERCU

Preface

In December 1978, Vietnam was intent on stopping Cambodia's genocidal Khmer Rouge regime. So it invaded its neighbor to the southwest. During February and March 1979, China, Cambodia's ally, came to its aid, invading Vietnam from the north. Every day, my sister and I, ages 7 and 4, clung to each other and wept as we watched the news. In the provinces of Cao Bang and Lang Son, Chinese soldiers were killing little children. They bayoneted pregnant women and forced them to run until they died of their wounds. To keep my sister and me from being raped or kidnapped, my mother cut our hair short and disguised us as boys. The Vietnamese forces were split, fighting the Khmer Rouge in the south while defending against the Chinese invasion in the north. We lived in terror that the invaders would attack Hanoi and Ho Chi Minh City.

The Chinese were aiming at Hanoi in the hope that Vietnam would rush back to defend its home and quit the fight against the Khmer Rouge in Cambodia. But luckily for my sister and me, fierce resistance by the Vietnamese army, combined with the difficult logistics of supplying the invading forces, stalled China's offensive.

The Chinese army had very nearly won the day by applying "Besiege Wei to Rescue Zhao," one of thirty-six ancient stratagems known as the *Wisdom of the East*. The People's Liberation Army rightly believed that by forcing Vietnam to fight on multiple fronts, it could divide and weaken the Vietnamese force. And yet, China failed to besiege Hanoi, because knowledge of the thirty-six ancient stratagems had long since spread throughout East Asia. Thus, Vietnam's leadership, well aware of "Besiege Wei to Rescue Zhao," had fortified Hanoi with a strong and experienced army along the Sino-Vietnamese border. Moreover, the Vietnamese troops successfully counterattacked the People's Liberation Army by using two more of the thirty-six ancient stratagems. First, they used "Lure the Tiger Away from Its Mountain Lair" to draw the enemy far from its position of strength. Then, using "Entice the Enemy to the Roof and Remove the Ladder," they cut off its supply routes.

The thirty-six ancient stratagems were compiled during a turbulent era of Chinese history: predominantly during the Warring States period and the Three Kingdoms period. They convey tactics on how to navigate and triumph in ever-changing situations. And even though they have been around for over two and a half millennia, these timeless stratagems continue to be applied with great success in business, politics, and international diplomacy today.

In my business of analyzing effective individuals, corporations, startups, and even mom-and-pop businesses, I have discovered in EVERY successful case the application of one or more of the thirty-six ancient stratagems. While we see them applied in varying degrees in the West, the stratagems have formed the very foundation of strategic thinking for East Asian businesspeople including Chinese, Japanese, Korean, Taiwanese, and Vietnamese. The Chinese have a saying: "The marketplace is a battlefield." The Japanese say, "Business is war."

The Chinese multinational company Lenovo is an apt example of how the thirty-six stratagems are adapted for achieving goals in business contexts, including market-share growth, negotiations, global expansion, mergers and acquisitions, and political maneuvering. Referring to the battle against Dell for personal computer market share in 2004, Liu Chuanzhi, founder of Lenovo, had this to say:

"Today we have a rather clearer understanding of who Dell is. We are taking this blow well. It has cleared our heads, turned us away from blind self-confidence. To sum up: Study Dell. Learn from Dell. Then send the troops out to beat Dell. We will see what the outcome is." Today, Lenovo is a global player in personal computers, mobile phones, servers, and cloud services.

In January 2014, at my Chinese-language class in Atlanta, Georgia, I told my classmates the news of this book's coming release. My Korean, Japanese, and Chinese classmates all could recite the thirty-six stratagems cold, whereas my German and American classmates had never heard of them and were fascinated by this "newfound" school of thought. In East Asia, children read the military classics the way North American and European children read fairy tales; politicians and businesspeople read them for strategy and tactics; scholars read them for wisdom; and ordinary people read them for entertainment. But whatever their motivations for reading about these ancient stratagems, EVERYBODY knows them.

I have read many excellent books on the ancient stratagems, most of them written solely from a historical or anthropological researcher's perspective. This book takes a different approach. While researching the literature in several languages, I strive to bridge the gap between Eastern and Western mind-sets by sharing my personal experiences, as well as searching out the personal narratives of people I have known or met. This book is a three-year-labor of passion. It organizes information from all the sources into a practical structure and boils them down to concrete take-away lessons. Every stratagem has a brief Chinese historical anecdote. Pertinent modern business cases follow, with concrete application tools laid out. The discussion of each stratagem ends with questions to reflect on so that you can implement the stratagem most appropriately in your own business situation.

Are you feeling stuck in your own conventional paradigm, unable to see through the filters of "the way things are done"? Has your business exhausted all the workable tactics you can think of? Are you not fully exploiting the opportunities of an ever more fluid business environment? The driving purpose for writing this book is to help business professionals come to grips with these questions—and use the results in ways they might never have dreamed of otherwise. The timeless wisdom in this book will help you free your creative thinking and outsmart the competition. It will help you do these things and more:

- Discover unconventional strategies and tactics, and adapt them for your business success.

- Implement specific strategies to free your thinking and gain the competitive edge.

- Stretch your current thinking to find new solutions to complex, fast-breaking situations.

- Adapt and apply strategies and tactics to unleash creative, innovative thinking.

- Unlock your "Asian mind" to discover the wisdom of the East.

Table of Contents

Introduction

In Chinese culture, thirty-six stratagems, or tactical maneuvers, have been handed down almost since time immemorial. Commonly referred to as the "wisdom of the East," these stratagems have spread and influenced other Asian cultures wherever Chinese thought, philosophy, and trade have gone. In Vietnam, where I grew up, children are exposed at an early age to the strong influence of Chinese culture. Originally oriented toward military exploits, the thirty-six stratagems are now associated mostly with Asian history, art, and popular culture, such as movies and soap operas. Although these stratagems originated in the East, we often see them applied universally, to varying degrees, throughout the world's history—in politics, economics, and human interactions in every sphere.

HISTORICAL BACKGROUND

The identities of these stratagems' authors are forever lost in the mists of time. In fact, they are really a compilation of stories from hundreds of Chinese warriors and strategists. "The 36 Stratagems" was first mentioned in the *Nan Qi Shu* (History of the Southern Qi). The Southern Qi Dynasty lasted from A.D. 479 to 502. The chronicle includes a biography of the political figure Wang Jingze, who mentioned "the 36 Stratagems of Master Tan." Master Tan (d. A.D. 436) was a renowned general serving the Southern Song Dynasty. It is said that by using these various stratagems, Master Tan saved his army from being destroyed. But there is no evidence that he is the author of the stratagems. If not the author, he may simply have been the one who compiled and applied them to good effect. The thirty-six stratagems may well have been in existence for over two thousand years.

The modern versions of the thirty-six stratagems are extracted from a tattered book discovered at a roadside vendor's stall in

Szechuan in 1941. It is a reprint of an earlier, handwritten book dating back to the late Ming or early Ching dynasty, entitled *The Secret Art of War: The Thirty-Six Stratagems*. A reprint was first published for the general public in Beijing, in 1979. Since then, several Chinese- and English-language versions have been published in China, Hong Kong, and Taiwan and then later in Germany and the United States.

THE STRATAGEMS

The entire text of the stratagems consists of only 138 Chinese characters. Most of the expressions are written in four-character or three-character idioms. The stratagems are divided into six chapters. The chapters, in turn, are defined into six different military situations, to which the stratagems apply. The first three chapters generally describe tactics for use in advantageous situations, whereas the following three chapters are more suitable for disadvantageous situations. The text of the thirty-six stratagems has been attributed to Sun Tzu's *The Art of War,* and to a degree, it also reflects some principles of Lao Tzu's *Tao Te Ching*. The three texts convey similar stratagems on how to navigate and conquer in ever-changing situations. The stories took place in the most turbulent era of China's history—predominantly the Warring States period and the Three Kingdoms period.

The Warring States period (475 B.C.-221 B.C.) began at a time when the numerous small city-states of the Spring and Autumn period had been consolidated into seven dominant states and a few minor enclaves. These states were Han, Wu, Zhao, Chu, Qi, Yan, and Qin. The friction between the seven states did not stem from anarchy or diplomatic reasons, but from greed and the lust for power, and it resulted in a time of endless brutal wars. It was all about one state trying to conquer its neighbors and consolidate power, claiming that China needed to be united as one and that the turmoil could end only with one state annexing all into a single empire.

The kingdom of Qin, in the northwest, finally conquered the southeastern kingdom of Chu in 223 B.C. The last opponents were conquered two years later, thus creating the Empire of Qin (China). This dynasty did not last long. After the death of Qin Shihuang (the self-proclaimed "first emperor") in 210 B.C., his successor held the Qin empire together for only a few years. The ruling family of Han then took control of the former Qin empire, and thus began the Han Dynasty.

The end of Han Dynasty started the Three Kingdoms period, when the kingdoms of Wei, Shu, and Wu vied to succeed Han in forming a new ruling dynasty. The Three Kingdoms period is one of the bloodiest epochs in China's history, with countless battles fought among the three rival states. The latter part of this period was marked by the collapse of the tripartite status quo, starting with the conquest of Shu by Wei (A.D. 263), the overthrow of Wei by the Jin Dynasty (265), and the conquest of Wu by Jin (280).

The thirty-six stratagems are familiar not only to Chinese but also to other East Asian peoples, including Koreans, Japanese, Taiwanese, and Vietnamese. Schoolchildren from these countries proudly recite them as poems, and businesspeople refer to them as a strategy playbook.

Chapter 1: Superior Stratagems

The "Superior Stratagems" are used in situations when one is in a superior position and resources or conditions are advantageous. Here are the stratagems:

1. Deceive heaven to cross the sea.

2. Besiege Wei to rescue Zhao.

3. Kill with a borrowed knife.

4. Conserve energy while the enemy exhausts himself.

5. Loot a burning house.

6. Clamor in the east, strike in the west.

Chapter 2: Opportunistic Stratagems

The "Opportunistic Stratagems" are used in situations when one can exploit the enemy's vulnerabilities. These are the stratagems:

7.   Create something from nothing.

8.   Sneak through the secret passage of Chen Cang.

9.   Observe the fire on the opposite shore.

10.   Hide a dagger behind a smile.

11.   Sacrifice the plum tree to preserve the peach tree.

12.   Steal a goat along the way.

Chapter 3: Attacking Stratagems

The "Attacking Stratagems" are used in situations when one is in a superior position and resources are to one's advantage. However, these stratagems are applied specifically when one seeks victory through direct attack. Here are the stratagems:

13.   Hit the grass to startle the snake.

14.   Borrow a corpse to resurrect a soul.

15.   Lure the tiger from its mountain lair.

16.   Release the enemy to recapture him.

17.   Toss out a brick to get a jade.

18.   Disband the enemy by neutralizing its leader.

Chapter 4: Confusion Stratagems

The "Confusion Stratagems" are used to confound the enemy and throw him off his guard to gain time for escape:

19.   Remove the firewood from under the pot.

20.   Muddy the water to catch the fish.

21.   Slough off the cicada's golden shell.

22. Shut the doors to trap the thief.

23. Befriend the far and attack the near.

24. Borrow a road to conquer Guo.

Chapter 5: Deception Stratagems

The "Deception Stratagems" are used to baffle and mislead the enemy:

25. Replace the beams with rotten timbers.

26. Point at the mulberry tree while scolding the locust tree.

27. Feign madness while remaining smart.

28. Entice the enemy to the roof, and then remove the ladder.

29. Deck the tree with false blossoms.

30. Make the guest become the host.

Chapter 6: Desperate Stratagems

The "Desperate Stratagems" are reserved for only the gravest situations. The tactics could be dramatic and unconventional:

31. Use a woman to ensnare a man (the beauty trap).

32. The open-city scheme

33. The double-agent ploy

34. The self-injury scheme

35. Linking stratagem

36. The escape ploy

ETHICAL CONCERNS IN MODERN BUSINESS APPLICATION

For Westerners, there may be some ethical or even legal concerns on the literal application of the thirty-six stratagems. Whether you use the stratagems or not, it is important to be aware of them so that you recognize situations where the competition might use them *against you.* This is not to suggest, however, that the Western world never operates cunningly or unconstitutionally. Rather, the stratagems frequently do come into play in the West as well—though generally without the awareness that they belong to an ancient body of wisdom.

In adapting the thirty-six stratagems to business, remember that the stratagems were conceived in a military context, where war is a zero-sum game and winning is not just the main objective but the *only* objective, whatever the cost. Even though the Chinese have the saying "The marketplace is a battlefield," this doesn't mean that the stratagems are to be applied literally in today's business world. Common sense still must prevail. We have a Constitution, laws, and ethical codes of conduct for good reasons, and those who violate them usually suffer the consequences. The strategic thinking in this book is like a sword: it is useful, but it cannot itself do evil. The constructive or destructive outcome stems from the good or evil in the mind of whoever wields it.

In the new globalized economy, to be unaware of the mind-set and behavior of people across the world puts you at a disadvantage. On the other hand, familiarity with the thirty-six Chinese stratagems will allow you to use them to your advantage, help you avoid destructive traps, unleash your creative thinking, and give you a competitive edge.

CHAPTER 1

Superior Stratagems

Stratagem 1:
Deceive Heaven to Cross the Sea

False perception leads to distracting actions.

Normality slackens vigilance.

An open situation hides secrecy.

—The 36 Stratagems

LONG AGO IN CHINA

The Emperor of the Tang Dynasty was asked to send his troops to support a small country in Koguryo (one of the three kingdoms of Korea). After setting out, the emperor was hesitant to move forward, for Koguryo was across the sea, a thousand miles away. Fearing that the emperor might withdraw, Xue, the general of his army, cleverly informed him that a wealthy farmer had invited the troops to his tent and promised to provide food for the journey. Delighted with the auspicious news, the emperor led his troops a few miles to see the farmer. The tent was festively decorated and full of servants bringing sumptuous food and wine. The emperor and his men spent a couple of days in the tent, enjoying the music and food without being aware that they had been led to the shore. (An arrangement of ten thousand canvases hid the ocean from view.) Hearing the whistling wind and the pounding of waves, the emperor opened the curtain to find that the entire army was on the open sea, heading for Koguryo. Faced with this fait accompli, he decisively continued the journey to the eastern shore.

When the ship safely reached the eastern shore, General Xue bowed to the emperor and asked his pardon for deceiving him. The emperor, impressed by his general's courage and shrewdness, rewarded him handsomely.

MODERN APPLICATIONS

Apple Culture

Apple is the acknowledged master in adapting the "Deceive heaven to cross the sea" stratagem. Even my unbiased, nonjudgmental 4-year-old, Levi, is entrenched in the Apple experience. He could stay in an Apple store for hours, having fun with the gadgets and all the cool stations. And as I said, he's *4*. When I attended a new-product launch at an Apple store in the Lenox Square mall in Atlanta, it felt like a red-carpet event. People waited in long lines—not complaining, mind you, but feeling lucky just to get their turn in the store! On launch day, the iPad sold more than 300,000 units. Within three days, the iPhone 4 sold 1.7 million units. It has been five years since the first launch of iPhone, but the excited buzz over Apple's products hasn't slowed down one whit. It's estimated that Apple could sell 7 million units of iPhone 5c and 5s, which launched in 2013, if they had enough supply. Most companies introduce a product or new brand with a regular launch—for instance, by posting or reading a press release. But Apple turns it into a dazzling, prestigious event or experience. This includes creating a truly eye-catching store design, delivering customer service like no one else's, and creating product buzz across the entire spectrum of media. As a result of Apple's masterful marketing strategy, customers and prospects feel a personal and emotional connection and deep loyalty to the brand and products. Apple doesn't sell a widget; it promotes an entire *culture*. In China and and Vietnam, building *guanxi* (relationship) includes the art of gift giving. Expensive brandies and luxurious accessories are now replaced by iPads or iPhones as gestures of modern relationship building. In Asia, where social status is an important cultural element, Apple's products represent a cutting-edge social status symbol.

Apple's success in launching a product lies in its relentless customer focus. Instead of talking excitedly about all the technical specs and features, Apple goes out of its way to emphasize the *benefits* and how the product affects customers and solves their problems. Apple gets everyone, including major media, technical bloggers, and individuals on social media, to talk about its coming product. Bloomberg news has repeatedly devoted an hour of air time to guessing what the new product may do, and CNN and Fox argue about Apple's revolutionary product features and benefits. Image sets Apple's products apart. The aesthetic style, status-symbol value, and stellar reputation inspire people to talk about it and show it off. What more effective marketing could there possibly be!

By masterfully "deceiving heaven," Apple has built a sterling reputation and implicit trust among its fans and potential customers, paving the way to "cross the sea" and sell even more products.

The Hospitality and Service Industry

I left Vietnam and immigrated to the United States in September 2000. I landed at Los Angeles airport and started my journey north along U.S. Highway 1, then headed across the country. The third day, we arrived in Las Vegas, the world-famous glitz-and-gambling haven that I had longed to visit someday. My husband and I are not gamblers by any stretch, but we had to try our luck with a few dollars on a slot machine in the Bellagio Hotel lobby. Before we knew it, we were late for dinner and the Celine Dion show that we had bought a package ticket for.

Casinos are a brilliant example of the stratagem's application.

In an environment full of noise and lights and garish colors and no clocks or windows, a customer loses track of time and reality. Everything about the casino—the games, arcades, shows, food, drinks, attractive women, shopping, and posh hotel rooms—is purposefully designed to make the experience pleasant and enjoyable. Losing money gambling seems somehow not all that significant.

The gaming industry has a way of drawing in its "customers" through the sensory experience it delivers, and then it creates a dependence on maintaining that experience. Here's an example of how its stratagem of "Deceive heaven to cross the sea" can work to devastating effect. Tan, a friend of mine who lived in California, lost his tech job when the dot-com bubble popped. While his wife worked more than twelve hours a day running her successful insurance business, he was bored. Looking for a mental challenge, he walked into the casino near his home. At first, he played for a couple of hours a day. Then gambling became a full-time job. When he had burned through his family's savings account, he stopped playing because he was out of cash. But the casino called him, offering him a credit line so he could keep gambling. A nice limousine picked him up, and the VIP treatment gave him back the self-esteem that he had lost since getting laid off.

Successful cruise lines and airlines also use the stratagem. A trip across the ocean takes a while, and it can get pretty monotonous. So a cruise liner offers a wide variety of activities and facilities: a gym, swimming pools, theaters, workshops, games, arcades, special-interest gatherings, restaurants, night clubs, and child care. Airlines have long understood the stratagem. Korean, Singapore, Cathay Pacific, and Arab Emirates provide a sumptuous experience with spacious seating, Internet, popular movies in a half-dozen languages, and attractive flight attendants bringing drinks and great food before you even thought to ask. For people like me, who frequently travel twenty-two hours one way between continents, this stratagem makes travel much less taxing—even enjoyable, to an extent.

An Example from Modern History

In 1965, Singapore declared its independence from Malaysia. In the same year, Great Britain was in the process of withdrawing from its colonies east of the Suez Canal, and in January 1968, it announced its official withdrawal from Singapore. Singapore needed to learn to survive on its own without any British military support.

In his memoir *From Third World to First*, Lee Kwan Yew, Singapore's first prime minister, recalls the time. Realizing that his tiny island country would be at the mercy of much larger Malaysia, Lee felt that only Israel—a small country with a strong army, surrounded by hostile countries—could help Singapore build a small but dynamic army. Lee told Goh, his finance minister, to call on Israel for help. But he was to keep the request on hold until Prime Minister Indira Gandhi of India and President Nasser of Egypt replied to his letters seeking their urgent help to build up the Singaporean armed forces. After a few weeks of waiting, India and Egypt congratulated Singapore on its independence but offered no military aid. Lee ordered Goh to push ahead in contacts with the Israelis.

Lee explained to Goh the need to maintain secrecy: they had to make sure that the Israelis' arrival did not become public knowledge, in order not to arouse opposition among the Malay Muslims living in Malaysia and Singapore. The residents of the small island, which has an area of about 670 square kilometers, are mainly Chinese. Living between the Muslim nations of Malaysia and Indonesia, they are effectively in the shadow of an overwhelming Muslim majority. Singaporean fears of a Malaysian incursion are an integral part of the two countries' history.

On November 24, 1965, the Israelis arrived in Singapore disguised as "Mexicans." In exchange for its invaluable military training, Israel insisted that Singapore officially recognize the nation of Israel and exchange ambassadors. But Lee insisted that he dare not anger the Malay Muslims in Singapore and Malaysia, who sympathized with their Muslim brothers the Palestinians as well as with Israel's other Arab neighbors. He was so adamant that Tel Aviv quit pressing the issue. When the Israeli presence in Singapore finally became public, Lee permitted Israel to establish a trade mission in 1968. In May 1969, Singapore upgraded the trade representative office to an Israeli embassy in Singapore.

Lee had masterfully applied "Deceive heaven to cross the sea." At first, to avoid upsetting Malaysia, Indonesia, and Singapore's Malay Muslims, Lee had Goh send letters to Prime Minister Gandhi of India and President Nasser of Egypt for help to build his country's armed forces. It was a gesture for appearance' sake, made with little confidence that either country would help. (Nor would their military strategy even be useful to a tiny army like Singapore's.) Their unwillingness to lend support gave Lee a valid, even compelling, reason to ally with Israel, without creating rancor among his Muslim citizenry or his country's Muslim neighbors. Then, to minimize the Israelis' exposure, they came disguised as Mexicans, whose presence would raise no quarrel with anyone in the region. Then Lee gradually introduced Singapore's relationship with Israel to the world by establishing a trade office. When Muslims in Singapore and the greater region had become accustomed to an Israeli presence, Lee allowed Israel to establish an embassy.

Changi Airport: The Entry Point Connecting Asia with the World

In 1995, my first business trip to Singapore was an eye-opening experience. Singapore was just a ninety-minute flight away from Vietnam, but it was already a highly developed, economically dynamic country.

My experiences at Singapore's Changi Airport are always pleasant. As the years go by, the experience gets more amazing despite my hectic travel schedule and the pull of jet lag. As soon as I land, I walk out into a light-filled walkway with a sky-high ceiling. I walk amid vibrant orchids, a butterfly garden, real tropical plants, and bright koi swimming in a cleverly designed pond. It gives me a sense of calm and pleasure—an unusual feeling since I am always stressed and in a rush at airports, especially in

New York, Los Angeles, and my hometown, Atlanta. An airport's purpose is to get people from one place to another. But Changi Airport has a greater purpose in a far bigger picture.

"Our vision is to connect lives," says Changi Airport Executive Vice President Foo Sek Min. "Airports are typically stressful places. Our goal is to remove the stress." Massage chairs, immaculate toilets, smiling employees, and great shopping make Changi the poster child for adopting the stratagem. Although Singapore is a small country, by "deceiving heaven," it has made Changi the seventh-largest airport in the world and "crossed the sea" with 47.5 million passengers in 2011.

Starting with this entry point, Singapore became the global hub for East Asia, attracting all the wealth, talent, and resources that the title implies.

Implementation Tactics

Let your plans be dark and inscrutable as night, and when you move, fall like a thunderbolt.

—Sun Tzu

Management of Service

"Deceive heaven to cross the sea" uses distractions to draw the target's attention away from what should be the main concerns. Distractions can take many forms, from creating comfortable or diverting environments to appealing to human emotions and desires, such the desire for self-esteem, social status, or trust. For Apple, Starbucks, and Whole Foods, the distraction is the event, the experience, and the community—and it leads the customer to a buying decision without too much concern about the price tag. In the case of airlines and cruise ships, the distraction is comfort and pleasure; the carrier brings the passengers to a destination in the greatest pleasure and comfort that is feasible. For casinos, the distraction is pleasure and illusion, geared to keep the customers inside playing, with nothing to remind them of reality or how much money they are losing.

Remember these key points:

- Rather than push a product, create an experience or event.

- Since brand appeals to emotional feeling and desire, emphasize the brand more than the product.

- Create a community rather than a need. Build a community around your product or service.

Change Management

People generally resist change because they fear the unknown, uncertainty, and the possibility of failure. To lure them out of their comfort zones, it is vitally important to make the change as unnoticeable as possible. General Xue cleverly introduced tent and food to entice the emperor and his troops down to the ocean. For President Lee to build the Singaporean army, he first disguised Israeli army consultants as Mexicans, then gradually introduced them to his people. In today's ever-changing world, providing proper communication and intensive training is critical to leading and managing change effectively.

- For managing organizational change, facilitate change little by little to avoid triggering drastic resistance and creating shock.

- For behavioral change, decide to work on one or two vital elements, which will create ripple effects to influence the related elements. Don't try to change everything at once.

Sales and Marketing

"Deceive heaven to cross the sea" is also widely used in sales and marketing when a market may be resistant to a new product or service because of price barrier or sheer novelty. For Singapore, building a tiny country into a global hub of finance and commerce starts with a pleasant entry point: Changi Airport. In marketing, a pleasant distraction or entry point might include any of these offerings:

- free trial period
- free shipping and liberal return policies
- bundled product and service to gain full buying commitment
- unbundled product and service to sell as a basic option with add-ons

Negotiation

In negotiation, use a fait-accompli tactic—that is, make it a "done deal." The fait-accompli tactic creates action. Once something is done, it is hard to undo; thus, the balance of power between the parties is altered.

QUESTIONS TO CONSIDER

✓ *What is your goal, product, or service, and what are the barriers to achieving the goal or selling the product/ service?*

✓ *What are your strengths? In what areas do you need assistance?*

✓ *What are the conventional activities in your environment that make it hard to achieve your goal or sell your product/ service?*

✓ *How can you break down your goals and blend them into the environment without being noticed?*

✓ *How will you plan your fait accompli?*

Stratagem 2:
Besiege Wei to Rescue Zhao

Avoid a head-on attack and wait until your enemy is dispersed.
Subdue your opponent indirectly by attacking his weak spot.

—The 36 Stratagems

LONG AGO IN CHINA

During the period of the Warring States, many small states fought each other, jockeying for position. In 353 B.C., the state of Wei launched a full-force attack on the state of Zhao. The king of Zhao asked the state of Qi for help. General Tian Ji led an army of eight thousand men to the rescue. Tian Ji wanted to attack Wei's army directly. But Sun Bin, his adviser, reasoned that there was no point in fighting head-to-head against the finest men in the Wei army, since Wei could easily crush them. Tian Ji took Sun Bin's advice and attacked the Wei state instead of its army. When the Wei army heard of the attack on their homeland, they rushed back to defend it. Returning home and exhausted by the forced march, they were ambushed along the way and defeated. Qi earned gratitude from Zhao, and fear and respect from Wei.

MODERN APPLICATIONS

Neighborhood Store Survives and Thrives against the Powerhouses

In an era of mega corporations, chain stores, and mergers and acquisitions, how could a local mom-and-pop retail store survive and thrive? An independent store cannot hope to compete on economies of scale and scope, yet it can differentiate itself by providing speed, convenience, personal touches, and a sense of community.

In my community of Marietta, Georgia, Big Peach Running Store is a mom-and-pop athletic-clothing store. It can't compete head-to-head with the giant retailers in the neighborhood, such as Footlocker, Payless, and Kohl's. So, to stand out, Big Peach Running offers very specific information and expertise for running enthusiasts and professional runners. Professionals consult with clients, helping them choose the best running shoes for their individual body, stride, and needs. Since childhood, I have long struggled with shoes because my feet are unusually wide for their length. Big Peach Running helps me find solutions for the pain I have dealt with for so many years. Free seminars on issues that concern runners (such as protecting knees, feet, and spine) are available. These are nonexistent in a chain retail store. The store is not only popular within the community; it's a destination for serious runners in Atlanta, twenty miles away.

These days, with a few clicks or keystrokes, anyone can see, compare, and buy anything from any corner of the world. Products and price alone no longer give the competitive advantage they once did. The store "besieges Wei" (offering expertise and consultation) to "rescue Zhao" (keep from be swallowed by giant retailers that are too big and cumbersome to provide the niche service).

Vintage Looks with a Modern Approach

Frantically scouting from one department store to the next in search of a new dress in a vintage style for a wedding I was attending, I thought about whether I could have one custom made for me, as I always did when living in Vietnam. Countless lovely styles were out there, but I was looking for something that told a story. A friend of mine pushed a few buttons on my cell phone and pointed me to ModCloth.com, where I could find a large collection of clothes and products of distinctive styles and looks.

According to Douglas MacMillan in Bloomberg Businessweek (August 13, 2013), Modcloth is a young start-up founded in 2002 by the husband-and-wife team of Eric and Susan Kroger. What sets them apart is their combination of art and science. She has a sense of style, and he's a tech guy. To "rescue Zhao"—to survive and thrive against giants like Amazon, which can sell all things to all people—small businesses have to focus on their niche. Modcloth uses customers' detailed feedback ("besieging Wei) to decide what items and clothing lines to stock, how to design its labels, and how to spot trends for future seasons—a feat too narrow and focused for the eight-hundred-pound gorilla Amazon to replicate. On top of its unique products, Modcloth has a deep knowledge of social media, which it uses to drive traffic and sales to its site. It is reported that 42 percent of visits to Modcloth are through mobile devices. The company's sales hit over $100 million in 2012, and it expects to grow more than 40 percent in 2013.

Mahindra & Mahindra versus John Deere

Coming to developed markets with a developing-market product sounds a little counterintuitive. Mahindra & Mahindra is one of India's biggest conglomerates. While it may be bigger than Deere & Company globally, it has just begun competing on Deere's U.S. home turf. Following the success of Hyundai Motors, which used unusually long product warranties to gain acceptance in the American auto market, Mahindra offers a five-year warranty on its small tractors in the United States, compared with the standard two years offered by Deere. To "rescue Zhao"—to avoid competing on price and fighting head-to-head against Deere and Osaka-based Kubota—Mahindra "besieged Wei" by rolling out many initiatives to distinguish itself from its competitors.

It focused narrowly on small tractors of up to 100 horsepower, launched a finance company that offered its American buyers zero percent financing with no money down for eighty-four months (versus Deere's zero percent interest for only 60 months), and rolled out a military appreciation program offering U.S. and Canadian veterans and their families two-hundred-fifty-dollar rebates. Bruce Einhorn and Siddharth Philip write in *Bloomberg Businessweek,* August 2013, that the U.S. market is part of Mahindra's strategy to build its brand awareness globally. By the end of 2012, the company had 8 percent of the U.S. market for small tractors—enough to rank it just behind Deere and Japan's Kubota.

Walmart's Synergistic Distribution System

Walmart enjoys the efficiency and economy of scale through its distribution system—a competitive edge that is the envy of businesses in and outside the retail industry and is hard for even Target to replicate. For starters, Walmart was one of the first retailers to build automated distribution centers, linked by computers both to its stores and to its suppliers. It has more than twenty in designated areas around the country. Second, all stores in a given area share warehouse space and coordinate their supply schedules so that they can share the same truck fleet, reducing the cost of keeping their stores stocked.

Sam Walton states in his memoir, *Sam Walton: Made in America,* that it takes the competition about five days to place an order and receive the replenishment. It takes Walmart two days. Not only does it reap rewards in flexibility and time, but the cost savings set Walmart apart. According to industry statistics, it costs a retailer from 4.5 to 5 percent to get the goods to its stores, whereas Walmart can get the same goods delivered for about 3 percent. By allying with its suppliers and combining its own forces among designated Walmart stores, the company makes its competitors, such as Kmart, Target, and many other retailers, fight on multiple fronts, and it beats them out on price.

IMPLEMENTATION TACTICS

"Is there a stratagem that can use one to attack ten?"
asked the king.

"Yes. Attack the enemy's weak point: attack the enemy where
he least expects it," replied Sun Bin.

"If the enemy prepares for a frontal attack, his rear will be weak;

If he defends his rear, his front will be fragile.

If he strengthens his left, he will weaken his right.

If he strengthens his right, his left is ignored.

If he tries to prepare in every direction,
he will be weak everywhere!"

—Sun Tzu

This stratagem advocates that in a competition, you need not fight head-on to win. In an ever-changing and dynamic business environment, you can find the enemy's weak spots and attack them, since no enemy can be present everywhere. To compete against the eight-hundred-pound gorilla Amazon, Modcloth exploits a customer-feedback system that allows it to tailor vintage and designer clothes to the customer's need—a trick that Amazon is too big and cumbersome to pull off. To enter the U.S. market, Mahindra focuses narrowly on selling small tractors in a market that Deere ignores or underserves. To survive in a community surrounded by big-box retailers, Peachtree Running makes itself indispensable with expertise and personal consultation.

Keep these points in mind:

- Avoid fighting head-to-head; instead, find your competitor's weak point.

- Rather than try to match up against your competitor, define *your* competitive advantage.

- Sell your products and services where the competition is underserving or ignoring the market.

- Create a niche that is hard to replicate.

"Besiege Wei to Rescue Zhao" also advises using an ally or combining forces and pushing your competitors to fight on multiple fronts. Thus, you can divide and weaken their forces. In Walmart's case, by joining forces with its suppliers and consolidating the schedules of Walmart stores in a designated area, it shares shipping costs, saves time, and leverages the information it gets to manage inventory. We can sum it up this way:

- Form an ally to increase the force you can bring to bear.

- Build a central hub to support a designated area.

- Divide the competition's forces by making them fight on multiple fronts.

QUESTIONS TO CONSIDER

✓ *Who are your competitor's rivals? What other party or element could affect the party you influence?*

✓ *What is your unique strength? How do you establish your core strength? How do you use it?*

✓ *Which markets and services are your competitors ignoring? How can you fill the void?*

✓ *Which section of the market is being underserved?*

Stratagem 3:
Kill with a Borrowed Knife

*When your enemy's situation is clear and
your ally's stance is uncertain, entice your ally to
destroy your enemy, thus preserving your strength.*

—The 36 Stratagems

LONG AGO IN CHINA

In the Warring States period (476-221 B.C.), King Zu had a prime minister, whose name was Nang, and three assistants. One of the assistants, Fei, was jealous of his coworker Buo, because Buo was the king's favorite assistant. One day, Fei told Prime Minister Nang that Nang was invited to a party at Buo's home. He then told Buo that Prime Minister Nang was coming to drink and dine at Buo's house. Buo naturally felt honored, and Fei offered to help him with the preparations. In China, it is customary that the host honor his guest with a gift. Buo knew that Prime Minister Nang already had everything from beautiful ladies to priceless jades, so he asked Fei for advice on what to give Nang. Fei suggested to Buo the recently captured arms of Wu, noting that Prime Minister Nang had a passion for fine weapons and armaments. He also advised Buo to arrange the weapons outside the entrance to his home so that Nang could see them when he arrived. Buo thanked him profusely and ordered his men to arrange the best and most powerful weapons, covered with a large sheet of cloth, outside the entrance to his house.

On the day of the party, when Prime Minister Nang was ready to attend, Fei rushed to the prime minister's house to inform him that armed troops were awaiting his arrival at Buo's house and that he should be cautious. To sow discord between them, Fei added, "Since Buo won the battle against Wu, he has gained favor and influence with King Zu. Everybody but you knows that he has been eyeing your position." Then he confided, "I myself have been on guard against him." The prime minister sent a confidant to Buo's house. He came back, verifying that the weapons were indeed at Buo's gate. Furious, the prime minister arrested Buo. Buo realized that Fei had set him up, and out of despair, he took his own life.

MODERN APPLICATIONS

Alibaba Survives the Dot-com Crash

In 1999, Jack Ma founded Alibaba.com (now the Alibaba Group), a privately owned Chinese group of Internet-based businesses, including business-to-business online Web portals, online retail and payment services, a shopping search engine, and data-centric cloud computing services. In 2012, two of Alibaba's portals together handled 1.1 trillion yuan ($170 billion) in sales—more than competitors eBay and Amazon.com combined.

Success did not come without its challenges. Because it overextended itself during the Internet bubble, Alibaba.com was not spared during the ensuing dot-com crash. In her book *Silicon Dragons*, Rebecca A. Fannin states that in January 2001, Alibaba's operating cost was $2 million per month, and it had cash reserves of less than $10 million. Jack Ma knew that he needed to take drastic action to rescue the sinking ship. He appointed Savio Kwan, a former GE top executive in China, as his chief operating officer. Kwan was assigned the painstaking and brutal task of stemming the negative cash flow. He implemented layoffs, gave the remaining staffers the ultimatum of having their salaries cut in half while tripling their stock options in the company, and adopted the GE culture of 20-70-10: weed out lowest-performing 10 percent, identify the 70 percent that are average performers to train and move them up the rung or push them out, and reward the star performers. This is something radical to the deeply rooted subsidized economy in China. Kwan also spent time with the management to talk about building a company culture, finding the right business model, and developing a top sales force. Jack Ma could have made the dramatic job cuts and other radical changes himself, but only at great cost to the morale and spirit of his remaining employees.

By using a borrowed knife—his newly recruited COO—Ma was able to implement the brutal job cuts without demoralizing the remaining people at Alibaba. When being interviewed, the employees thought it was the right strategy to rescue the company. In 2005, their morale and confidence were so high, they were ready to take on the world. And did they ever! In 2006, Alibaba's market share skyrocketed, whereas Ebay Eachnet (Ebay in China) shut down its site and officially withdrew from the Chinese online auction market.

The Marriage of Korean Lotte and Vietnamese Bibica

The marriage between the local Vietnamese confectioner Bibica and Korea's Lotte Confectionery Co. Ltd. has turned sour during the past five years. When joining forces with Lotte, Bibica expected multifield cooperation between the two partners, in everything from management know-how to transferred technology, to distribution. But Lotte seems determined to turn Bibica into its subsidiary, with Bibica making only products that enhance Lotte's brands, rather than the other way around.

Bibica's case has injected a note of caution into many other businesses planning to sell stakes to foreign partners. Inexperienced local businesses have learned a bitter lesson when they not only didn't get the cooperation and support they expected, but got taken over instead. It could be that a foreign company "borrows a knife" by partnering to take advantage of the existing distribution network, only to take over and "kill" the local brands.

Joint ventures can be mutually beneficial for both the foreign and the local partner. The foreign company gets its foot in the door, benefits from the local expertise on laws and regulations, and enjoys the existing distribution network while the local partner acquires transferred technology, management know-how, and global exposure. But in many cases, the multinational corporation takes over and makes all the high-impact decisions while using the local partner as a dummy. Or vice versa: the local partner takes the opportunity to acquire transferred technology, management skills, and international exposure while the foreign partner plays the role of "gentle giant."

Samsung Electronics: "Killing" with Borrowed Technologies

In 1969, when Samsung began, it had no technological capability. A decade later, Samsung Electronics could do assembly only, with key components made in Japan, and when it started to produce its own goods, many were of terrible quality. For example, when it produced electric fans, they were so poorly designed and manufactured that the fan's neck would break if the unit was not lifted with two hands. Gradually, by "borrowing" technology from other companies, Samsung Electronics began improving its production. In 1974, the company entered the semiconductor business, but it faced huge challenges due to lack of technical know-how and poor quality management. It teetered close to bankruptcy until founder Lee Byung-Chul brought in Japanese semiconductor engineers to transfer technology to his own Korean engineers. When the business stabilized in the 1980s, Mr. Lee chose to specialize in electronic memory.

According to Sea-Jin Chang's book *Sony vs Samsung*, Samsung bought 64K dynamic random-access memory (DRAM) technology from the U.S. semiconductor company Micron. It recruited Korean engineers with education and work experience in the United States to learn the technology, tweak it, and develop 256K DRAMs. It established a U.S. subsidiary with an R & D center and prototype production facilities, to train high-potential Korean engineers. After training in the States, the engineers returned to Samsung Semiconductor's Korean facilities to create products that surpassed those of their U.S. counterparts. In 1987, Samsung succeeded in developing 256K DRAMs. By "borrowing a knife"—multiple technologies and know-how from the United States and Japan—Samsung Electronics now had the capability to "kill." In the 1990s, the number of U.S patents held by Samsung Electronics had increased dramatically, and in 2004 it had a higher ratio of patents to investment than Sony.

Nike Borrows a Knife (and Cuts Itself)

Nike's successful business model of outsourcing its manufacturing is the ultimate application of the "kill with a borrowed knife" stratagem. By 2005, over 700 factories manufactured footwear and clothing for Nike around the world. Nike lists 124 plants in China contracted to make its products, 73 in Thailand, 35 in South Korea, 34 in Vietnam, and others elsewhere in Asia. It also produces goods in South America, Australia, Canada, Italy, Mexico, Turkey, and the United States and employs 650,000 contract workers worldwide.

In addition to taking advantage of the ultracheap labor costs in developing countries, the company avoids direct liability regarding labor laws or complicated legal structures in different countries. After costs rose and labor organized in Taiwan and Korea, Nike urged its subcontractors to move their manufacturing to Indonesia, China, and Vietnam. And indeed, all the plants making Nike products in Vietnam are owned and run by Taiwanese and Korean businesspeople. Meanwhile, Nike spends the money it saves on labor and legal expenses in Southeast Asia on aggressive marketing campaigns. Nike and other sport companies often pay hundreds of millions of dollars to sports stars such as Tiger Woods and Michael Jordan for product endorsements.

But in 1991, when activist Jeff Ballinger published a report documenting low wages, terrible working conditions, and other abuses in plants producing the company's products in Indonesia, Nike discovered that the borrowed knife had a double edge. Max

Nisen reports at BusinessInsider.com (May 9, 2013) that a CBS interview with Nike factory workers provoked mainstream media attention and became a national issue. More abuses emerged, especially in contracted plants in Vietnam. In 1997, Nike opened new Niketown retail stores, only to see increasing protests. College students across the United States began demonstrating and boycotted Nike products. Nike was being shamed in public to the point where its badly tarnished company image was hurting sales. Facing weak demand and unrelenting criticism, the company realized that it needed to change. In May 1998, a real shift began when then-CEO Phil Knight announced that Nike would raise the minimum age of workers, significantly increase contractor workplace monitoring, and adopt U.S. OSHA clean-air standards in all factories. In 2005, the company published a detailed 108-page report revealing conditions and pay in its factories and acknowledging widespread issues, particularly in its Southeast Asian factories. As of this writing, it continues to post its commitments, standards, and audit data as part of its corporate social responsibility reports.

Nike has managed to turn its image around by bringing its contracted factories into line. And yet, the April 2013 factory collapse in Bangladesh, which killed over a thousand workers, is a reminder for those in the industry who outsource: learn the lessons from Nike and others, and be cautious and vigilant when applying the "kill with a borrowed knife" stratagem.

IMPLEMENTATION TACTICS

We cannot enter into alliances until we are acquainted with the designs of our neighbors. We are unfit to lead an army on the march unless we are familiar with the country's geography—its mountains and forests, its valleys and precipices, its marshes and swamps. We shall not be able to turn natural advantage to account unless we use local guides.

—Sun Tzu

Expanding Business

The stratagem is used when one wants to enter a fierce competition and does not have enough strength to ensure victory. Seek out stronger partners and temporarily "borrow" their strengths to achieve your goals or "kill" your competition. Nike's borrowed knife is outsourced manufacturing; Samsung's is borrowed U.S. and Japanese technologies. This stratagem could be take many forms:

- Use local partners, subcontractors, and joint ventures to get through local bureaucracies and avoid direct liability issues.

- If you are a local business, use licensing, franchising, or joint ventures as your borrowed knife. On your own, you may not have the brand awareness and marketing power that these arrangements can provide.

- Use others' strengths, through cooperation or a joint venture, to acquire transferred technology, management know-how, and exposure.

- Use an established brand to enter a new market.

Dissociating Yourself from the Deed

Companies also "kill with a borrowed knife" to implement drastic change such as layoffs and restructuring. This is important because, if the company were to carry them out directly, it could demoralize its employees or related parties and create unnecessary resentment. CEO Jack Ma of Alibaba hired a COO specifically to take care of the layoff, allowing Ma to dissociate himself from the deed. This stratagem can also be handy in mergers and acquisitions when the buyer wishes to dissociate itself from the takeover. It is also useful for companies that do not wish to be embroiled in local legal and political wrangling. Nowadays, many multinational corporations use third-party contract workers for cost savings and legal protection.

- Use consultants or assign emotionally detached parties to deliver bad news, change initiatives, restructure, and handle layoffs.

- Use a third party to handle contract workers

- Use a third-party company to handle a merger or acquisition.

Business Networking

- Associate yourself with the image and brand you wish to build.

- Join a reputable organization or high-level association to tap into resources and gain influence.

- Volunteer and involve yourself in high-profile or cross-functional projects at work or in the community to gain exposure and create new leads and contacts.

- Surround yourself with resourceful people (think tank, mastermind group, professional association).

QUESTIONS TO CONSIDER

✓ *What is your plan to move into higher-level associations?*

✓ *What are your weaknesses?*

✓ *Who in the market can provide you with the needed abilities that you lack?*

✓ *How can you make use of their strengths?*

✓ *Whose influence would help you?*

✓ *Whom do you need to influence?*

Stratagem 4:
Conserve Energy While the Enemy Exhausts Himself

To subdue the enemy, it is not necessary to make a direct attack. Use the weak force to maneuver him into exhaustion; in the process, his strength is impaired, and your force is reserved intact.

—The 36 Stratagems

LONG AGO IN CHINA

In Stratagem 2, Sun Bin used "Besiege Wei to rescue Zhao" to defeat Pang Juan, commander of the Wei troops. When the Wei heard of the attack on their hometown, they rushed back home to defend it. Now that Sun Bin had the army of Wei attacking him to defend its own territory, he feigned retreat. On the first night of the retreat, he ordered 100,000 fires lit. On the second night, he ordered 50,000, and on the third night, only 30,000.

Pang Juan, believing that Sun Bin's troops were deserting in droves, led the Wei army on a forced march for two days to capture Sun Bin and the remnants of his army. With clever calculation, Sun Bin located where two days' forced march would bring the Wei army: it was in the middle of a ravine. On a tree in the ravine, Sun Bin carved, "Beneath this tree dies Pang Juan, by the command of Sun Bin."

As the Wei army arrived at the ravine and Pan Juan tried to discern the words by torchlight, Sun Bin's army launched volleys of arrows. Hit with arrows, Pan Juan slit his own throat with his sword.

MODERN APPLICATIONS

Negotiate on Your Home Turf

Lam, a friend of mine, is a self-made millionaire. He started a liquefied petroleum gas bottling business and soon distributed to the whole south of Vietnam. Aspiring to expand his business to China, he was introduced to a group of Chinese gas distributors in Beijing. After a typical first meeting, the Asian businessmen reconvened at a fancy restaurant, where a lavish seven-course meal with unlimited liquor was served. Lam, mindful that he was on his guests' turf, refrained from the binge drinking. His Chinese counterparts, on the other hand, were not pleased to see him stop after a few rounds of *kan pei*(bottoms up). Lam soon found himself out of the conversation among the Chinese men, who now spoke Mandarin among themselves despite his presence. They talked, joked, and laughed among themselves in Mandarin until Lam picked up the signal. He had no choice but to join in the drinking until one older Chinese host said to him in English, "Now I like you. Let's do business."

Entertaining the other party is serious business in East Asia. Having foreign counterparts fly to their home turf, savvy negotiators wear them out with long waits and lengthy negotiations with various groups, departments, and delegates. While creating an environment to build *guanxi* (relationship) and remove barriers, such nocturnal activities as eating, drinking, and karaoke also further contribute to the exhaustion of the Western or other foreign counterparts, who, along with being jet-lagged, are unfamiliar with the food, customs, language, and tactics.

Samsung Forges Ahead while Sony Labors

In the early 1990s, Samsung was still perceived as a manufacturer of cheap, low-quality televisions and air conditioners. Not anymore. The company is taking the world, including the U.S. market, by storm. In the past two years, on recent business trips in Seoul, Vietnam, and even the United States, I have observed dynamic marketing campaigns building Samsung as a young, hip, and innovative brand. In September 2010, I walked into the Intercontinental Hotel in Ho Chi Minh City to witness the grand Galaxy red carpet event. While upbeat music played, attractive promotion agents where celebrating the launch of the Galaxy mobile phone. The experience was every bit as exciting as a launch event in New York City.

From humble beginnings as a food-processing and noodle company in 1938, Samsung entered the electronics industry in the late 1960s, and the construction and shipbuilding industries in the mid-1970s. Since the 1990s, it has increasingly globalized its activities and electronics, particularly semiconductors and mobile phones, while overhauling its image as an innovative world-class brand.

First, Samsung Electronics borrowed technologies from the United States and Japan to produce DRAM, tweak it, and make a product that surpassed the competition. Meanwhile, Sony's vision and mission have always focused on innovating a unique and original product, which is extremely costly and time consuming. Sony had invented cool products including the Walkman, digital cameras, PlayStation, PS Vita, and Aibo. But innovative products tend to be inefficient, hard to commercialize, or late to a fast-changing market. Being the late entrant with limited innovation and know-how compared to Sony, Samsung invests heavily in marketing to build brand awareness while focusing its resources on developing the mobile phone, a de facto fashion item.

Sony, meanwhile, is weak in digital technology. Its brand value is established organically from the company's track record in innovation and new-product development. Sony was not quick enough to capture the digital technologies, while Samsung was. While Sony labors to conceive new products and commercialize them, Samsung conserves its resources for marketing and speedily developing mobile telecommunication.

According to Sea-Jin Chang, back in 1997, Sony's analog TV dominated the market when it introduced WEGA, which applied flat cathode-ray tube technology and solved the problem of distorted images near the edges of the television screen. It was so successful and so popular with consumers that Sony failed to foresee the new trend and embrace the next-generation technology. Having believed that next-generation liquid crystal display (LCD) and plasma display panel (PDP) technologies were hardware and commodities that could be quickly and efficiently supplied by external sources, Sony instead invested in developing organic light-emitting display (OLED). Meanwhile, Panasonic focused on PDPs, Sharp on LCDs, and Samsung Electronics on both. The philosophy of always developing unique and original technology held Sony back in many ways. It had difficulty commercializing OLED technology because of several technical issues; meanwhile, its competitors introduced PDP and LCD televisions and made hefty profits. In 2002, the demand for these products soared while Sony suffered from a shortage of flat panels because it relied on an external source and didn't have its own production line. In 2003, Sony had to set up a joint venture with Samsung Electronics to secure a reliable supply of flat panels. And in 2005, it had to expand the joint venture by devoting an additional $2 billion to building large LCD flat panels. Samsung has cleverly adopted the stratagem "Conserve energy while the enemy exhausts himself." It *conserved energy* and resources to focus on greater, more immediate gains while Sony *exhausted itself* conceiving new technologies and playing catch-up because it failed to predict the trend.

IMPLEMENTATION TACTICS

The stratagem advises, instead of confronting the enemy directly, to wait and watch the enemy and bring him down when he is at his weakest. It also says to develop the ability to identify the new battleground; then move first, set up your position, and wait for the exhausted enemy to come. Sony was occupied and drained by its innovation ideology while Samsung focused its efforts on marketing its brand. Meanwhile, the ability to foresee the new trend in LCD allowed Samsung to move first, set up its defensive position in the market, and await an exhausted Sony.

Remember:

- Run your competitor around. Tire him out.

- Wield your patience against those with no patience.

- Keep your opponent constantly tense, occupied, and depleted by constant distracting movements and activities. When he exhausts himself, bring him down with a final blow.

- Develop the ability to spot the new trend (identify the new battlefield), predict the timing, and pounce when the opportunity arrives.

Negotiation

- Lure your counterpart out of his comfort zone.

- Wear him down with distracting activities.

- Watch him struggle till his mind is foggy and his will waivers; then ask him to make a decision. He will be more prone to concede and give in.

- Watch for the clues, or tells, to when a counterparty is in crisis or at least uncomfortable.

QUESTIONS TO CONSIDER

✓ *What events or conditions might cause the battlefield to shift?*

✓ *What shift in the battle may create new opportunity for you?*

✓ *What can you do to acquire even a slight edge over your competition?*

✓ *What actions can you take to prepare for the opportunity and seize it in a timely fashion?*

Stratagem 5:
Loot a Burning House

When the enemy is in crisis, exploit his misfortune and attack in full force. This enables the strong to conquer the weak.

—The 36 Stratagems

LONG AGO IN CHINA

In 498 B.C., Gou Jian, king of Yue, led troops to fight against an attack from Fu Chai, king of Wu. He was bitterly defeated by the much stronger enemy. To save his army and state, he agreed to be Fu Chai's slave.

For three years, Gou Jian, his wife, and his men served with dedication and loyalty as Fu Chai's slaves. As a result, they were released. While gradually rebuilding and strengthening his state, Gou Jian did not forget to pay homage to Fu Chai by sending him gold, money, and beautiful women—all the while working on his dream of revenge.

Ten years later, the opportunity finally came. The state of Wu suffered a fierce drought, resulting in famine for Fu Chai's people and army. Influenced by corrupt officials, Fu Chai executed his right-hand man, who had been his most loyal and intelligent adviser. Then, in 482 BC, a desperate Fu Chai led his best men to Huang Chi to meet rulers from the surrounding states and ask for support, leaving behind the old and weak. Seizing the opportunity, Gou Jian led his 50,000 men to attack Fu Chai's weakened army and brought down the state of Wu.

MODERN APPLICATIONS

Gouging at Universal Studios; Free Umbrellas in Singapore

On Christmas 2012, my family took a trip to Universal Studios in Orlando, Florida, so the kids could visit the Harry Potter theme park. While we waited in line for over three hours to get to Hogwarts Castle, a few drops of rain fell. Immediately, park employees were on the spot, selling disposable ponchos at eight dollars apiece. Despite the rain, I was steaming. The ponchos were nothing more than orange trash bags with a hole for the head, and I had no choice but to buy four of them. By taking advantage of the weather, the park squeezed a lot of money from its captive market, but it sure left us all with a bad taste in our mouth. Then I remembered being in Singapore for a business meeting in 1998. We were walking on the street in the afternoon when it started pouring rain. At once, umbrellas and raincoats were available at every retailer along the street—for free. It has been over fifteen years, but that rainy day in Singapore is still fresh in my memory. I believe the Singaporean government has a brilliant strategic application of the "loot a burning house" stratagem. The Singaporeans don't make immediate money on the raincoats and umbrellas—indeed, they lose a little—but they enhance their and their nation's brand, building trust and sowing seeds of return tourism, more commerce, and expanded global influence.

Foreign Manufacturers Loot China's Baby-Formula Market

In 2008, China had its first tainted-milk scandal, with others popping up in the years after. Six infants died of severe kidney damage, and an estimated 300,000 babies suffered from kidney stones after drinking tainted formula. The formula from several major Chinese dairy companies was found to contain melamine, a poisonous additive that falsely boosts the protein levels in milk. In December 2011 and July 2012, two Chinese companies recalled baby formula containing high amounts of aflatoxin, a carcinogen produced by certain molds in cows' feed. In late 2013, another company issued a separate recall after "unusually high" levels of mercury were found in its main line of infant milk formula. Because of this, Chinese consumers have lost trust in local brands and have increasingly been looking to imported brands. Taking advantage of the panic among Chinese parents, foreign baby-formula manufacturers have fixed their prices. It is reported that the price of imported formula rose 30 percent since the beginning of the tainted-milk scandal. The Chinese government investigated and charged that the manufacturers had artificially inflated the price of formula. It fined five foreign companies for "looting" the troubled baby-formula market in China.

The Diva of Distress

Lynn Tilton, a self-made billionaire, claims herself the "Diva of Distress" and the "Wild Woman of Wall Street." She is the owner of Patriarch, a company that specializes in buying ailing or distressed manufacturing companies and turning them around. As a ruthless, smart Yale-educated single mom with experience in the trenches of Wall Street, she got rich buying up distressed industrial companies that no one else seemed to want. According to the *Forbes* April 2011 issue, she also claimed that she saved manufacturing jobs in America. She owns and finances pieces of seventy-five companies, including Stila Cosmetics, Howard Hughesfounded MD Helicopters, and mapmaker Rand McNally. Through structured financial vehicles, her company, Patriarch, has picked up the distressed debt of dozens of enterprises across North America and rebundled them into so-called collateralized debt obligations. Her company also makes money from fees by serving as collateral manager of various kinds of funds.

IMPLEMENTATION TACTICS

When the enemy is thrown into disorder, crush him.

—Sun Tzu

Business Investment

The stratagem "Loot a burning house" advocates capitalizing on crisis and exploiting chaotic business situations, seizing the advantage by darting into the "burning house" situation and "looting" while more timid—or less prepared—souls tend to back away. Crisis may give birth to opportunities for clever investors and business professionals. The opportunities arise in many forms. Stock market fluctuations, financial crises, political turmoil, and real-estate bubbles are good examples of chaotic situations in which lucrative business opportunities may include buyouts, takeovers, real-estate investment, and either long or short stock positions.

- Watch for chaotic situations, and take advantage of individuals and companies in turmoil, when you can buy them or their products/services at a bargain.

- Exploit and profit from temporary market distortions, macroeconomic transitions, and political uncertainty.

- Look for ailing or distressed companies to buy cheap. If the business doesn't pick up, strip the assets and liquidate them for cash. If the business is promising, restructure the company and turn it around.

- Seize the opportunity at the moment when your competitor is most vulnerable.

- Create turmoil and chaos to wear down your competition.

Service Management

This stratagem can also be used to good advantage in its positive connotation—that is, by *not* looting a burning house. This is especially true in customer service. You can effectively influence your customers when they are at their most vulnerable. Singapore won me over by lending me what I needed: an umbrella. The benefit to a company's (or a nation's) goodwill is everlasting. It may not improve the immediate bottom line as Universal Studios did by "looting" the poor customers trapped in the rain, but the long-term profit in image, goodwill, and influence is priceless.

- Lend a helping hand when your prospective customer is vulnerable or in need.

- Find opportunities to serve your customer when the competition won't. You will win lifelong loyalty.

- Take a leadership role in crisis, since that is precisely when leadership is most influential.

QUESTIONS TO CONSIDER

✓ *Who is experiencing a crisis?*

✓ *What can cause crisis and turmoil for your competitors?*

✓ *What opportunity can the crisis create for you?*

✓ *How do you foresee the opportunity and take advantage of it when it arises?*

✓ *In what way can you use others' capital/resources for your venture?*

Stratagem 6:
Clamor in the East, Strike in the West

In any battle, the element of surprise can provide an overwhelming advantage. Even when face to face with an enemy, you can still use surprise by attacking where he least expects it. To do this, create an expectation in the enemy's mind through the use of a feint.

—The 36 Stratagems

LONG AGO IN CHINA

During the reign of Emperor Jing of the Han Dynasty, a rebellion broke out among seven states, including the states of Wu and Chu. General Zhou Yafu was ordered to capture the rebels. He built up a great wall in the path of Wu army, preventing the rebels from moving northward, and cutting off their food supply.

The Wu army was trapped. They feigned an attack on the Han army at the southeast end of the wall, but General Zhou Yafu was not fooled. He ordered his troops to be well prepared at the east end for the real attack. When the Wu army attacked at the east end, the Han repulsed them, and they beat a hasty retreat. Seizing the opportunity, Zhou ordered his best soldiers to launch a real attack in the West. By then the Wu army was exhausted and was easily defeated.

MODERN APPLICATIONS

Spirit Airlines: You Fly Cheap; Your Bag Doesn't

Keeping the kids busy for seventeen days of winter break is

costly. After a couple of short trips, we decided that a cheaper way was to spend a week in Miami. Digging around, we found Spirit Airlines and bought a great package of four round-trip Atlanta-Miami tickets and five-day car rental for $1,050. As of this writing, Spirit Airlines, a leader in ultralow-cost air travel, has grown 150 percent in the past year. Looking at the November 2013 traffic results, Spirit outperformed other U.S. legacy airlines, including Delta and American. It generated a load factor of 83.7 percent compared to Delta's 79.4 percent and U.S. Airways' 82.4 percent. Load factor is a key airline metric indicating the percentage of a plane's seats with passengers in them. A high load factor is a good sign that the carrier is matching demand, or revenue passage miles, with capacity additions or available-seat miles.

Being an ultralow-cost airline enables Spirit to increase its market share faster than is possible in most industries. But how can it be profitable? Here's the secret: if you value customer service, Spirit Airlines is probably not for you. In fact, you get no customer care whatever. If you need it, you pay a fee. Spirit recently announced that it will no longer offer its customers a toll-free customer service number. On the flight, my two rambunctious boys were thirsty. I paid three dollars per bottle of water. And it's fifty dollars for a carry-on bag. I always want to sit near the front of the plane because I tend to get motion sickness. On Spirit, I have learned to get accustomed to sitting near the tail since the front would cost me an extra two hundred dollars per seat. And make sure you have your boarding pass printed in advance—printing one at the airport will cost you ten dollars.

Spirit Airlines uses "Clamor in the east, strike in the west" skillfully. While promoting the ultralow-cost fare (clamoring in the east), it charges outrageous fees (strikes in the west) for even the most basic services and needs, including luggage, water, and customer care. They haven't yet put credit-card scanners on the restroom doors, but we'll see.

Bundles and Freebies

- When the iPhone 5 was first released, I bought one for $125 instead of $800 by signing a two-year cell phone contract. The cell phone companies practically give away the devices, then tie the customer up with a two-year service contract.

- Bank and credit card companies stress "no fees" in certain areas but charge high interest rates and high fees on overdrafts.

- Amazon gives away free or low-priced e-books on Kindle to push the Kindle product. I bought a Kindle for the abundant choices of inexpensive or free e-books.

- Each week, grocery stores sell one or two items as loss leaders to lure customers and build traffic, resulting in sales of higher-priced items.

- Google develops areas not only to leverage its brand but also to create diversions so that Microsoft must "fight on multiple fronts": Gmail versus Hotmail, Google Docs versus Microsoft Office, Google Chrome versus Internet Explorer. This weakens Microsoft's efforts to pit Bing against Google search, which is Google's bread and butter.

IMPLEMENTATION TACTICS

Weakness comes from having to prepare against many possible attacks; strength, from compelling your rival to make these same preparations against you.

—Sun Tzu

This stratagem hinges on the principle of diversion, which is commonly used in warfare. You feign an attack on one quarter, and when the enemy's attention is diverted, you strike where he least expects the attack. Wee Chow Hou and Lan Luh Luh suggest in their book, *The 36 Strategies of the Chinese*, that in business, the stratagem is often applied in mergers and acquisitions. By concealing one's true intentions, a buyer can avoid paying a jacked-up price, bidding against competing companies, or getting unwanted attention from media and regulatory bodies.

Canny salespersons often use the stratagem cleverly to influence a buying decision. When a customer is paying attention to a particular benefit or feature of a product, she may let her guard down in examining other areas. The seller can generally make more profit on these areas when the customer's defenses are relaxed. Spirit Airlines is an example, using ultralow-cost airfares to entice the customer in. Then, when the customer relaxes, the airline launches the full attack by collecting outrageous fees on everything else.

Negotiation

- Develop questioning techniques. Ask people questions that have nothing to do with your concerns, while staying alert for inadvertently leaked information related to your concerns.

- Develop negotiation techniques. Concede something that is unimportant to you, and make a big deal of it. The other party may then reciprocate with a concession of something you really want.

- Use the stratagem to conceal your true intentions.

QUESTIONS TO CONSIDER

✓ *How do you unbundle your products and services?*

✓ *How do you charge for extras?*

✓ *What action do you take to feign a false attack while launching a real attack somewhere else?*

✓ *What do you do to reinforce your competition's belief in your false attack?*

CHAPTER 2

Opportunistic Stratagems

Stratagem 7:
Create Something from Nothing

Create a false front to conceal your real intentions.
When the enemy takes the bait, switch the false front
with something real. Thus, your enemy is put into
confusion. Now it is time to launch an attack.
—The 36 Stratagems

LONG AGO IN CHINA

In A.D. 755, during the Tang Dynasty, General Zhang Xun had a small army and limited resources to fight against the rebels. He commanded his men to make a thousand life-size straw dummies and dress them in black. As night began to fall, the dummies were tied to ropes and lowered over the wall. The rebel troops, thinking the enemy was mounting an attack against them, unleashed a volley of arrows. When they realized it was a scam, they had already wasted thousands of arrows. Then Zhang Xun commanded five hundred real troops to descend the city walls during the night. Thinking Zhang Xun was using the same old trick, the rebels ignored them. The five hundred soldiers attacked the rebels' camp by surprise and defeated them.

MODERN APPLICATIONS

Pho 24: From Street Dance to Elegant Ballet

Squatting on a tiny stool on a narrow sidewalk and slurping a steaming bowl of pho noodle soup in the sultry tropical heat is part of Vietnamese life. Pho, a concoction of chicken or beef broth with rice noodles and a variety of herbs and spices, is served morning, noon, and evening in thousands of street stalls from one end of Vietnam to the other. In 2003, on my first trip back to Vietnam after immigrating to the United States, I could not help but be intrigued by the idea of enjoying pho in a stylish air-conditioned restaurant in the most exclusive area of Ho Chi Minh City. Pho, the "street dance" of Vietnam, had been transformed into elegant ballet.

Ten years later, in December 2013, I had the opportunity to interview Trung Qui Ly, founder of the Vietnam-based Pho 24 franchise, which is enjoying success in over sixty outlets in Vietnam and over twenty more in the Asia-Pacific region, including Indonesia, Singapore, Japan, South Korea, and Australia.

Weathering countless barriers including exorbitant commercial real-estate rents, high inflation rate, and lack of management know-how, Pho 24's revenues in Vietnam reached $20 million in 2010. Its flagship stores are located in the high-end retail areas, among elite-brand stores such as Movado, Gucci, and Chanel. When jokingly asked how many bowls of pho a store had to sell each day just to make the rent in such expensive neighborhoods, Ly replied that thanks to the added value of the prestigious locations, his restaurants charge three times as much as the street stalls, and the fast table turnaround in the bustling commercial districts makes his business model sustainable.

Ly has created a new business model. Pho 24 successfully positioned itself as a healthy fast food that serves the rapidly rising middle class in Vietnam and Asia, where customers still have very deeply rooted culinary tastes yet also like the image of a modern, Westernized lifestyle.

Creating a Billion-Dollar Trade from Trash

Americans have the saying "Bad for Jill is good for Jack." Adam Minter stated in *Bloomberg Businessweek*, August 29, 2013, that thousands of tons of metal, worth millions of dollars, leave the United States for China each year. Johnson Zeng, one of the traders, spends a million dollars a week on low-grade scrap for export to China. China accounts for 43.1 percent of global demand for scrap metal. Low-grade scrap requires significant work—manual, chemical, or mechanical—to turn it into copper clean enough to be melted in a furnace. Because recycling low-grade scrap requires a lot of manual labor, in America the demand is too low and labor costs are too high to be worth it. For China, America is the world's most attractive source of scrap. Zeng has created a fortune out of scrap metal, creating something from nothing.

From Flower Arrangements to Edible Arrangements

When my friend Joe bought a fruit-bouquet franchise, I had the opportunity to learn more about the business model of this young company founded by Pakistani brothers Tariq and Kamran Farid. The company offers 150 arrangements designed for every occasion, including chocolate-dipped strawberries, flower-shaped pineapple, and honeydew melon carved in race-car shapes. In 1986, Tariq was still in high school when he bought a failing flower shop in their East Haven, Connecticut, neighborhood with a five-thousand-dollar loan from a family friend. With hard work and help from his mother, the first store not only survived but thrived, becoming four stores.

When Tariq was still a child in Pakistan, his father brought home big baskets of fruits every day. During the days at his flower shop, Tariq began experimenting with a fresh idea: arrangements of fruit instead of flowers. Unable to get a loan for such an untested idea, he launched Edible Arrangements from a section of that first flower shop.

One day, a customer walked in and asked the brothers if

they would consider opening a fruit-bouquet store near his home in Boston. After designing the computer systems, training manuals, production and profitability tracking, and supply chain management process, Tariq and his brother, Kamran, launched the first franchise in 2001. As of 2012, the business had grown to more than 1,100 stores globally, with 2011 revenue of $422 million.

The Kardashians' Empire

Visiting DASH fashion store, founded by the Kardashian sisters, is a treat every year when my family and in-laws get together in Miami. The store is always busy with visitors despite the limited parking. My nieces and I once drove up and down Collins Avenue to find a parking spot, then could barely get into the store because of the long waiting line. The stores have expanded from Los Angeles to Miami and New York thanks to the prominent success of the sisters' television series *Keeping Up with the Kardashians*.

Before becoming a household name, Kim was just a California girl next door. She began her fashion venture as shop girl and built a clientele selling clothes to high-end boutiques. Soon enough, she was invited to red-carpet events with her famous friend Paris Hilton and started to garner media attention. In 2007, Kardashian came to prominence after a sex tape with her boyfriend was leaked. In October that year, the Kardashian family was cast in the new series *Keeping Up with the Kardashians,* which portrayed a chaotic life of equal parts drama, train wreck, and fantasy. Its huge success has led to the creation of spin-offs. The Kardashian series has lasted over six years. Even though the concept would be iffy to a lot of us, the family has skillfully turned its exposure into a lucrative marketing and branding machine. Kim has seventeen million online fans. According to the *Hollywood Reporter,* in 2011 the Kardashian family's various business ventures, including clothing, perfume, shoes, shopping memberships, and nail polish, are said to be worth $1 billion. The Kardashians are the masters of "Create something from nothing."

Being and Nonbeing of a Dot-com

The concept of *xushi* (being and nonbeing) is depicted nowhere better than in Michael and Xochi Birch's story, as featured in *Fortune*'s November 2010 issue. As social network pioneers, their perfect timing came when every media giant wanted to buy a social-networking site in early 2008. The couple created Bebo.com and sold it to AOL at a hefty price of $850 million. But AOL failed to capitalize on Bebo's pioneer position, which Facebook quickly took over. AOL recently sold the site to some private investors for less than $10 million. As Lao Tzu said, "Being and nonbeing give birth to each other." Our own being or nonbeing is up to us.

IMPLEMENTATION TACTICS

> *"Being and nonbeing give birth to each other.*
> *Difficult and easy accomplish each other.*
> *Long and short define each other.*
> *High and low depend on each other.*
> *Before and after follow each other."*
>
> —Lao Tzu

In Lao Tzu's philosophy, what seems real can be unreal; what looks strong can be weak. We tend to believe what we want to believe. Psychologically, we tend to pay attention to evidence that agrees with our current beliefs, and ignore evidence that does not.

This stratagem is based in the scheme of deception. In Asia, the literal phrase "create something from nothing" can also have a negative connotation. The idea is to create a false impression to manipulate your competition. According to Lao Tzu, we can turn one situation to another by creating a perception, since perception is reality. In the business world, the stratagem is creatively adapted in many forms: leveraging bad PR for exposure, associating with high-level individuals or organizations to gain influence, creating illusion and perception to distinguish a brand, or starting a business with nothing more than a vision or idea. In many ways, the Kardashian empire is the ultimate example of adapting this stratagem.

Ralph Lauren is one of the pioneer fashion companies that set itself apart from the competition by creating an illusion of lifestyle. The Ralph Lauren brand is perceived beyond just the commodity of clothing, thanks to its projection of luxury lifestyle, image, and status. Moreover, unlike other luxurious brands, Ralph Lauren set different price points so that its products are accessible to different clienteles. This strategy enables the company to capture a broad market while maintaining the brand image.

Marketing and PR

- Create an illusion to give a placebo effect.

- Change people's perception by creating an illusion.

- Leverage bad media and rumors about your competition.

- Leverage bad media about *your* brand to gain exposure.

- Polish your presence, presentation, and communication skills to establish credibility.

- Create belief to lead people to a desired action.

- Establish fans and followers by projecting the right illusion or perception.

- Tag along with well-known names, personalities, associations, and organizations. It worked for Kim Kardashian.

- Avoid letting your product/service be treated like a commodity, by creating added value, differentiation, uniqueness.

- If you are not a thought leader, piggyback on great ideas or thoughts and give them a new twist.

- Strategically make your product or service public by associating with influential events, people, and organizations.

Business Start-up and Innovation

Starting a business and succeeding is never easy. But Ly of Pho 24 and the Farids of Edible Arrangements prove that one can create something from nothing by having an idea, working hard, persevering through obstacles, and continuously add value.

- Think beyond the accepted bounds of what can be done, and you can make the impossible possible.

- Create added value, differentiation, and uniqueness.

- Add one idea or a new player, and give the old game a twist to change the rules or create a totally new game.

QUESTIONS TO CONSIDER

✓ *How do you differentiate yourself from your competition? How do you stand out in a crowd?*

✓ *What added value are you providing to your clients? What added value are you not providing?*

✓ *What research are you doing to be more attractive to your clients? What need is not being met? What are you missing?*

✓ *What one new player should you add to change the rules of the game or create a new game?*

Stratagem 8:
Sneak Through the
Secret Passage of Chen Cang

Pretend to expose part of your movement, and then launch a surprise attack somewhere else, where the enemy is not prepared to defend himself. So, in warfare be alert, and you can penetrate in all situations, like the wind.

—The 36 Stratagems

LONG AGO IN CHINA

In 208 B.C., at the end of the Qin Dynasty, Liu Bang was forced to retreat to Szechuan Province during a battle between himself and Xiang Yu. To make sure Liu Bang posed no further threat, Xiang Yu deployed General Zhang Han and his troops to monitor Liu Bang's movements. Liu Bang's army stopped at a place called Shu, which was surrounded by steep mountains and accessible only by wooden bridges. To prevent an attack from Xiang Yu's army and to put General Zhang Han's mind at ease about the possibility of his making an immediate counterattack, Liu Bang ordered his men to destroy all the bridges leading to the only road to Szechuan.

Weeks later, when Liu Bang was ready to march to central China and even the score, he openly had his soldiers repair and rebuild the destroyed bridges. While the wooden bridges were gradually being restored, General Zhang Han, with his soldiers on the other side, was ready for Liu Bang's retaliation. But he could see no sign of Liu Bang's forward movement even though most of the bridges were restored. General Zhang Han found out too late that Liu Bang had used the restoration of the bridges as a decoy to trick him. While his soldiers labored away on the bridges, Liu Bang had led his strongest men secretly out of Shu via a small hidden passage called Chen Cang, launched a surprise attack, and defeated General Zhang Han's army.

MODERN APPLICATIONS

Using "Chen Cang Passage" for Industrial Espionage

As the author of this book, it pains me to confess that even with all my understanding of the thirty-six stratagems, I fell into a cunning application of "Sneak through the secret passage of Chen Cang." I was once asked to deliver a leadership retreat program for three hundred people at a European company that has manufacturing facilities in Vietnam. Because of the nature of the group, I needed to completely customize the content and work with managers of the company to create a package from scratch. After holding several meetings and working with my team in the States, I developed unique content together with a simulation for three hundred participants. I was excited to send them the detailed proposal that our team in the United States, including a Six Sigma expert and a game-and-simulation expert, had collaborated on. Upon receiving the proposal, the company was apologetic—it would not be able to execute the grand plan this time but hoped to cooperate with me in the near future. I later found out that the invitation to deliver a highly customized program for them was their way to "sneak through the secret passage of Chen Cang." After collecting U.S. know-how and detailed information through our several meetings, they used our final detailed proposal as a blueprint to hire a local vendor, who could execute the already developed program at a much lower cost. My company's blueprint served as their Chen Cang passage, allowing them to sneak around us and use a cheaper local vendor.

Negotiations, bidding, and so-called joint ventures are widely used for industrial and information espionage in the modern business world. A Japanese company once carried out numerous negotiations with a potential partner in the Chinese province of Anhui, but the joint venture never materialized. Secretly using the negotiations, the Japanese figured out the production secrets of high-quality Xuan paper, which is used for traditional calligraphy and painting. The Chinese lost their unique know-how to the Japanese, who are known today for manufacturing the highest-quality Xuan paper in the world.

Dr. Phil: Influence with a Purpose

In 1995, Oprah Winfrey hired Phil McGraw's legal consulting firm, Courtroom Sciences Inc., to prepare her for the Amarillo, Texas, "beef trial." He impressed her so much that she invited him to appear on her show. His appearance was so well received by viewers that she invited him onto her show weekly. Later, he launched his own syndicated daily television show, *Dr. Phil,* and a series of best-selling books on self-help and diet. He is known for his authoritative, commonsense manner and, above all, his candor. His packed audience is hungry for advice and absorbs whatever he has to say. According to Pat Winger's article in *Newsweek* magazine, before Thanksgiving 2012, McGraw mentioned Mike Moreno's book *The 17-Day Diet* on his show twenty-seven times and meticulously explained how to buy the book (which was available only on its own Web site). What he did not mention was that his son, Jay McGraw, was the book's publisher and that they both had a financial interest in it and its spinoff products such as a video, a foreign-language version, and *The 17-Day Diet Cookbook.* Finally, on the show in January, about two months after he had gotten his viewers to embrace *The 17-Day Diet,* he revealed his son as the publisher of the book.

Uninitiated viewers would not know that Dr. Phil had used the "secret Chen Cang passage" (his influence) to "sneak past" his audience and capitalize on the lucrative field of diet books.

Today, mainstream and reality-show celebrities are used

extensively in marketing. The public is interested in the celebrities' lives and follows them through social media, and the celebrities exploit their followers to make more money. Companies and promoters pay them to write sponsored tweets and blogs on what they wear, where they eat, what they drive—you name it. Online, they can be paid as much as ten thousand dollars to write a sponsored tweet. Unlike in traditional advertising, the stratagem works effectively here because celebrities use their fame *secretly* to endorse products without the public's awareness.

IMPLEMENTATION TACTICS

To obtain victory, one should vary his plans according to the enemy. Enticing the enemy into battle, one may appear as shy as a young maiden. Then, when the enemy shows arrogance, one must move as fast as a hare and catch him by surprise.

—Sun Tzu

This stratagem has much in common with "Clamor in the east, strike in the west." It advocates diverting the enemy's attention and striking when and where he least expects it. The one distinction is that this stratagem dwells on the interplay between opposite elements such as night and day, and the "open" and the "dark." It is used extensively in martial arts and a wide range of sports, including soccer, football, and basketball. In the *Book of Stratagems,* Harro Von Senger suggests the first two:

- Hide your sophisticated intentions behind an apparently harmless action.

- Mask an uncommon intention behind commonplace deeds or words.

- Use public relations and infomercials when you engage in an activity, charity, or social event to promote your brand or raise awareness of it.

QUESTIONS TO CONSIDER

✓ *What conventional stratagems or tactics does your rival expect you to use?*

✓ *What unconventional stratagems or tactics do you have available to you?*

✓ *How do you make your rival believe that you will resort to conventional tactics?*

✓ *What outcome do you expect when you use unconventional tactics?*

Stratagem 9:
Observe the Fire on the Opposite Shore

When disorder and conflict break out among the enemy's forces, wait patiently while the bad situation builds up. When conflict intensifies, the enemy's strength is weakened and he begins to self-destruct. Seize the opportunity to conquer with minimal effort.

—The 36 Stratagems

LONG AGO IN CHINA

During the Three Kingdoms period, Cao Cao applied this stratagem against the two brothers Yuan Shang and Yuan Xi, who were his rivals. Pursued by Cao Cao, the two brothers decided to flee to Liaodong with a force of several thousand men. Cao Cao knew that the lord of Liaodong had a deep hatred for the Yuan family because of past issues with the brothers' father. The brothers hoped only to find temporary shelter in Liaodong, Then, when the opportunity presented itself, they would eliminate its lord and use Liaodong as a base from which to kill Cao Cao and expand their rule over northern China.

Learning of the plan, Cao Cao's general advised him to take the opportunity to kill the Yuan brothers and conquer Liaodong. Cao Cao calmly smiled and said to leave the Yuan brothers and the lord of Liaodong to their own devices. He predicted that if he kept pursuing the brothers, they would persuade the lord of Liaodong to join forces with them against him. But Cao Cao would rather create conditions under which the Yuan brothers and the Lord of Liaodong turned against each other. And so Cao Cao refrained from marching on Liaodong.

When the forceful and merciless Yuan brothers sought his assistance, the lord of Liaodong found something suspicious about them. He knew that the brothers had always intended to take Liaodong but had been too occupied with defending themselves against Cao Cao. Still, if Cao Cao attacked Liaodong, he would have no choice but to join forces with the Yuan brothers and defend Laodong. But if Cao Cao did not attack him, he knew for certain that the brothers would eventually seize Laodong by force. So when he realized that Cao Cao was not going to send his soldiers to attack Liaodong, he had the Yuan brothers beheaded. Acknowledging that his army was no match against Cao Cao's, he sent the Yuan brothers' heads to Cao Cao as an offering of peace.

MODERN APPLICATIONS

Samsung Observes the Fire on Sony's Shore

According to Sea-Jin Chang, Sony has long viewed middlemen such as dealers, wholesalers, and distributors as costly and inefficient. For one thing, its consumers already looked specifically for Sony products when shopping in stores. Also, after building a strong brand and securing innovative product development capabilities, Sony did not feel that it needed to motivate distributors to push its products. Its sales incentives for distributors were weak compared to those of its competitors, and it did not invest in strategic marketing and specific-product marketing. It started to rely less on traditional distribution channels and instead attempted to sell directly through online and Sony Style stores. Emulating the success of Dell's direct sales approach, Sony believed it could avoid the evil of middleman channels.

But Sony's direct-sales strategy faced serious conflict with its existing distribution channels. Not only external traditional distributors but also internal sales departments have been hostile toward Sony Style, the new direct-sales approach.

Samsung Electronics, on the other hand, reinforced its relationships with medium and heavyweight distribution channels. As an underdog, it understood the importance of having good relationships to fare better in price negotiation and market entry and penetration. In early 1998, after being rejected by Circuit City, Samsung built a close relationship with Best Buy. Using joint advertising, Best Buy at one point accounted for 30 percent of Samsung Electronics' U.S. sales revenue. In the old days, the quality of analog products of different brands varied widely. But now, since the quality of digital products is basically the same, consumers make buying decisions based more on customer service and promotional schemes provided by branded distributors such as Best Buy.

Sony's direct sales did not grow as fast as planned, and the Samsung brand has been strongly repositioned through big-box distributors as well as small distributors.

"Local Snakes" Watch the Fire on the Opposite Shore

In his book *The Lenovo Affair,* Ling Zhijun says that in early 2004, Lenovo was busy fighting an increasing squeeze from the powerhouses, or "tigers," in the high-end computer market. These included IBM, Toshiba, Dell, Fujitsu, and Hewlett-Packard. Meanwhile, "local snakes"—small local computer companies in the regional markets—were getting very strong and eating up Lenovo's market share. The local companies had long been enjoying watching the fight between the powerful tigers. The "snakes" were originally retailers of computer parts and then became computer-assembly companies. They somehow smuggled products into China by paying bribes, gradually built up assembly companies, and legitimized their service. After learning from branded computer makers, they established a standard for their own machines and set up servicing and repair systems. By May 2004, Lenovo's market share dropped to 21.3 percent. By "observing the fire on the opposite shore," the local computer makers had eaten up about 10 percent of the Chinese computer market.

Don't Jump on the Bandwagon

After the Vietnam War, relations were tense between Vietnam and the United States. As the United States imposed an embargo on Vietnam, Japan, meanwhile, invested there and enjoyed advantages as an early entrant in the foreign investment arena. Japan applied this stratagem quite often, most of the time sitting on the side, observing carefully and then taking advantage when a rival had a crisis. When the West joined forces to condemn China for the deadly government crackdown at Tiananmen Square, many countries pledged to stop doing business with China. Japan wisely did not jump on the bandwagon. On the contrary, Japanese businesses secretly opened up and approached China to establish rapport and build a business relationship.

IMPLEMENTATION TACTICS

Knowing the place and time of the coming battle, we may be able to concentrate from the greatest distances in order to fight.

—Sun Tzu

This stratagem suggests watching for the enemies to fight and deplete themselves, waiting for the moment when the enemy is at its weakest from the fight, then striking. Samsung did not jump on the bandwagon by joining Sony in its "kill the middlemen" strategy. Instead, it waited to see how the initiative worked with Sony while secretly enlarging and deepening its own relationships with distributors.

- A Chinese proverb says to "pit the two adversaries against each other; then you will win." Another says to "sit on the mountain and watch the tigers fight."
- Exploit the conflicts in the environment.
- Faced with uncertainty, adopt a wait-and-see attitude.
- Refrain from acting to wait for the right moment.

Strategic Thinking

A Chinese saying advises, "Build ships in a drought, and chariots in the event of flood." Conventional thinking would have us do the opposite: build chariots in a drought, and ships in the event of flood. The rationale behind the saying is that droughts and floods are erratic situations; they come and go. If you follow the conventional way, you will run into head-on competition since everyone is doing it. The Japanese refrain from jumping in and extinguishing the "fire" (as we instinctively do), to "observe" and take a strategic approach. Remember:

- Look beyond the immediate and obvious market situation.

- "Observe the fire" by taking note of customers' needs and reactions, and adjust your strategy accordingly.

- Don't be bogged down by the current event. Take into account how the market/customer will change after the fire, drought, or flood. Develop a long-term perspective.

QUESTIONS TO CONSIDER

✓ *What conflict is your competitor facing?*

✓ *How will you take advantage of your competitor's conflict?*

✓ *What is the current crisis? How does your competition react to it?*

✓ *What action do you take when taking into account the erratic reaction of the market?*

✓ *How do you see beyond the immediate to develop a long-term action plan?*

Stratagem 10:
Hide a Dagger Behind a Smile

Win the trust of your enemy to disarm him while secretly preparing an ambush. To win the war, prepare the ambush well and launch it when your enemy least expects it.

—The 36 Stratagems

LONG AGO IN CHINA

During the Spring and Autumn period, the ruler of Wu wanted to conquer the state of Hu. Instead of using a direct attack, he married his daughter to the prince of Hu as a gesture of goodwill and peace.

He gathered his ministers and asked, "Which state should we attack to expand our territory?" One minister suggested an attack on Hu. The ruler of Wu feigned fury and had the minister beheaded in front of everyone. The news spread quickly, and the ruler of Hu no longer doubted Wu's sincerity and treated the state of Wu as an ally. The ruler of Wu strengthened his army and destroyed the state of Hu in a surprise attack.

MODERN APPLICATIONS

Google, the Smiling Underdog

Yahoo started as a search site but soon evolved into a tremendously successful media company. Yahoo's strategic plan was to expand its online advertising expenditures, and search became a much lesser priority. This led to the outsourcing of its search services in 1996. Google, a young search enginefocused company, played the role of underdog as a supporter of Yahoo. It wasn't viewed as a threat and was ranked far behind more popular search engines such as AskJeeves and Alta Vista.

Despite the new position of strength that Google had attained, it still did not pose any threat to its partner and other major rivals, since the search business yielded only marginal profit. Playing the smiling underdog, Google created and fine-tuned Adwords, the pay-per-click model that was the payment standard for online advertisers. Around 2003, Google started to attract advertisers away from Yahoo and other major online media rivals. Yahoo terminated the contract with Google and purchased two online search companies, Inktomi and Overture, and decided to run search activities on its own. But by 2006, Google already dominated half of all online searches, using nontraditional but nonetheless exciting advertising models. By 2012, with a global market share of 65.6 percent, Google dominated the world in search and online advertising options.

The Strategically Humble Japanese

The Japanese are known for their pride in their supposed national superiority, and yet, at the same time, they appear humble and even meek. After the Second World War, when the China intervened in the Korean War, the Americans focused more than ever on rebuilding Japan. Japanese leaders realized that this was their golden opportunity to revive the nation. They kept a low profile and humble posture while catching up with the Americans, first in textiles, steel, ships, motorcars and petrochemicals, then in electrical and electronic goods, digital goods, and information technology. Feigning vulnerability, they posed no apparent threat to giant Western business competitors as they continued to improve their products by adopting and adapting Western technologies. Now Japanese products, including cars, electronics, home appliances, and high technology, are surpassing Western products in affordability, aesthetic appeal, maintenance, and efficiency.

Kaihan Krippendorff writes in his book, *Hide a Dagger behind a Smile*, that Japanese car manufactures continue to apply the "smiling" stratagem even as their success has alarmed American consumers. When the big three U.S. automakers, GM, Chrysler, and Ford, launched a "Buy American" campaign, the Japanese automakers countered the campaign by simply *being* more American. They opened manufacturing plants in the United States, creating jobs for American workers, and they have continued to reap profits by never dropping the smile.

The Smile in Hospitality and Retail Businesses

Surveys suggest that restaurant servers with pleasant personalities and nice smiles are rewarded with 25 percent more in tips than those without. Southwest Airlines, Singapore Airlines, Thai Airlines, and Disney differentiate themselves by acknowledging the power of a smile and practicing it religiously. To ensure an enthusiastic, smiling workplace, Southwest Airlines espouses the "Southwest spirit": celebrate everything, hire fun people, and entertain others. Zappos, one of the most successful online shoe retailers, creates the Zappos Way, which encourages fun and a little bit of weirdness. Amazon paid almost $1 billion to buy Zappos, not because Zappos sold the best shoes or had an excellent business model, but because Zappos had learned how to build the strongest customer-centric culture and customer relationships.

The Walt Disney Company is famous for excellence in customer service. In addition to training its own people for the past twenty-five years, Disney expanded its best practices to a global training and consulting service. Its clients range from the National Football League to public school systems. According to Disney vice president Jeff James, the most frequent initial request from companies hiring Disney is to train their frontline people to be as happy and smiling as Disney's. James says, "The key is getting senior leadership to embrace the business case for a strong customer experience, to show how it translates to the bottom line."

IMPLEMENTATION TACTICS

*Soft words and flattering expressions are
rarely paired with real humility.*

—Confucius

The stratagem suggests winning the enemy's trust and attacking him when he lets his guard down. By maintaining its smile before drawing its "dagger," a company can put the competition at ease while gathering enough strength to compete, just as Google has done with Yahoo and Microsoft. In the retail and service industries, the smile translates directly to bottom line. Zappos, Singapore Airlines, Disney, and Southwest Airlines are great examples of the stratagem adopted effectively. So remember:

- Convey a smile, confidence, and courtesy when conducting business, especially in sales and services. You will gain trust, making it easier to influence your prospect or customer.

- Use a smile to defuse an irate customer. By letting them vent, you solve their problem indirectly.

- When you are embarrassed, insulted, and speechless, calmly smile.

- Play the smiling underdog while you ready yourself for a day of fighting back.

- Establish, build, and repair the relationship with humility, smiles, apologies, and gift giving.

- Keep your friends close, and your enemies closer.

- Don't let the smile beguile you. Look behind it. It could convey genuine warmth or joy, or it could stand in for a lie, anger, embarrassment, sarcasm, or nervousness. You need to read the nuances and subtleties of the smile.

QUESTIONS TO CONSIDER

✓ *What customer service culture do you cultivate in your organization?*

✓ *What is your strategy for staying on good terms with your rival?*

✓ *What is your strategy for staying on good terms with the people in your organization?*

✓ *How "humble" are you?*

Stratagem 11:
Sacrifice the Plum Tree to Preserve the Peach Tree

*When loss is inevitable, make sacrifices
to gain potential victory.*

—The 36 Stratagems

LONG AGO IN CHINA

Le Lai Sacrifices Himself to Rescue the Leader

Most third-graders in Vietnam are familiar with the historical account "Le Lai Sacrifices Himself to Rescue the Leader." When I was young, my history teacher told me the story of the Vietnamese resistance against Ming-dynasty China during A.D. 1418-27. In 1419, the Vietnamese army, led by Le Loi, was surrounded. A servant named Le Lai asked Le Loi to give him his robe. He put it on and left the camp. The Chinese captured and killed him, thinking he was Le Loi, the resistance leader. Le Loi was able to escape and later went down in history as the founder of Vietnam's Le Dynasty. To commemorate the event, two streets in the bustling central metropolis of Saigon Vietnam, are named after Le Lai and Le Loi.

The Horse Races

During the Warring States period, General Tian Ji often held horse races with the prince of Ji. The races consisted of three heats, each with a different horse from each contestant's stables. Tian Ji lost regularly. One day, Sun Bin advised Tian Ji to run the first heat with his poorest horse against the prince's best. Then, in the second heat, he should use his best horse against the prince's second-best horse. Finally, in the last heat, he should run his mediocre horse against the prince's poorest horse. Tian Ji followed Sun Bin's advice. In the first heat, he sacrificed his poorest horse, which lost to the prince's best, but had a tie in the second heat. In the third heat, he won when his mediocre horse raced against the prince's poorest horse—a better horse than the one he had lost in the first heat.

Modern Applications

Jim Collins Hedges His Bets

Before becoming a world-renowned business guru, Jim Collins was teaching entrepreneurship and small-business courses at Stanford University. The pivotal moment of his career arrived when he started working on a project with Jerry Porras: the book *Built to Last.*

In an interview with *Success* magazine (Oct, 2013), Collins said, "I was at the fork in the road where I could hedge my bets and do a traditional PhD, become a traditional professor, which was highly probable, or bet on the piece of work that Jerry and I had produced." He confided that at that moment, he and his wife had nothing to fall back on if they should fail. But they were confident of the intangible education they had and the tremendous support they could count on from each other. Jim Collins and Jerry Porras embarked on an intensive six-year research project of studying the founding, growth, and development of exceptional companies that have stood the test of time, to uncover timeless fundamentals that enable organizations to survive and thrive. The book became a fixture on the *Businessweek* best-seller list for more than six years, starting in 1994.

Collins used the "Sacrifice the plum tree to preserve the peach tree" stratagem one more time when he took most of his money from *Built to Last* and invested in the book *Good to Great.* He says, "Instead of just banking it, we reinvested it into the next project and invested another five years of our lives." He spent any savings that would come from *Built to Last* on hiring researchers and organizing the team dedicated to the book project. The second book also became an international best-seller and was translated into thirty-five languages. "After that, everything changed," he says. As we can see today, Jim Collins is the world-renowned business author and thought leader whose books are devoured by business leaders everywhere and whose speaking fee is up to $100,000 per speech.

Jack Welch's 20-70-10 Principle

When Jack Welch was CEO of General Electric, he invented the 20-70-10 model. By emphasizing differentiation—ranking employees into performance categories of the top 20 percent, middle 70 percent, and bottom 10 percent and then managing them "up or out" accordingly—he believed that an organization could build meritocracies and continuously raise the performance bar, thus increasing a company's competitiveness.

Each year, he would fire the bottom 10 percent of his managers, develop the middle 70 percent with training and coaching, and reward the top 20 percent with bonuses and stock options. The middle 70 percent got close coaching and training to accelerate them to the top 20 percent; and, of course, some dropped into the bottom 10 percent and were out. Jack Welch earned a reputation for brutal candor in his meetings with executives. He closed factories, reduced payrolls, and cut lackluster old-line units. His public philosophy was that a company should be either number one or number two in a particular industry. If not, they should leave it completely. GE reduced basic research and closed or sold off businesses that were underperforming. It also outsourced a number of service businesses so that the company could focus on its core strengths. Welch's strategy was later adopted by other CEOs across corporate America and Asia.

In *Jack: Straight from the Gut,* Welch states that GE had 411,000 employees at the end of 1980, and 299,000 at the end of 1985. Of the 112,000 who left the payroll, 37,000 were in businesses that GE sold, and 81,000 were let go from continuing businesses. In return, GE had increased its market capital tremendously.

IBM to Let Hardware Business Go

In January 2014, IBM agreed to sell its low-end server business for $2.3 billion to Lenovo. For the past ten years, IBM has continued its transformation from primarily a hardware producer to a provider of services and software for businesses and governments.

Revenue at IBM's systems-and-software business, which sells mainframes, servers, and other hardware, declined 26 percent in the last quarter of 2013. The segment's gross margin is also getting squeezed. It fell 3.5 percentage points to 36 percent last year. Compared to an 89 percent margin for its software business, hardware was a low-margin business that IBM wanted to exit.

"This divestiture allows IBM to focus on system and software innovations that bring new kinds of value to strategic areas of our business, such as cognitive computing, Big Data, and cloud," said Steven A. Mills, senior vice president at IBM Software and Systems.

In 2005, Big Blue sold its PC division to Lenovo. Since then, IBM has shed other hardware units, including printers and retail-store systems. In the server business, where added value is no longer valid (since quality distinction between competing servers is insignificant), IBM had to fight on volume, which is not its strength.

Lenovo, based in China, has the opposite strategy. As the world's largest PC maker, it sells products on razor-thin margins, yet it makes money on volume. Acquiring IBM's server business is expected to help it weather the decline in its core personal-computer business and escalate competition against heavyweight players such as Dell and Hewlett-Packard.

IMPLEMENTATION TACTICS

Do not stay on desolate ground.

—Sun Tzu

This stratagem is effective when you operate under constraints of time, money, and resources. The ability to set priorities, let go, and make sacrifices is critical to gaining in the long run. The essence of "Sacrifice the plum tree to save the peach tree" is that it is not failure to quit the game you cannot win, so that you can focus your resources on the game where you can conquer. IBM let go of its hardware business to focus its resources on innovations in systems and software. GE closed out its underperforming businesses to focus its resources on becoming number one or two in specific areas. Jim Collins made a bet trading his traditional professorial career for something more profitable and exciting. Many Japanese, Singaporean, and Korean companies concede in industries where they are no longer competitive, so that they may thrive in others. Keep these points in mind:

- Focus on your most significant, most valuable strengths, and be willing to sacrifice those less significant.

- Let go of noncore areas to focus on your core business.

- Take a calculated risk for a bigger win.

- Let go of a product, service, or industry where you can no longer be competitive.

Sales and Marketing

"Sacrifice the plum tree to save the peach tree" is also applicable in sales and marketing. Linkedin, Netflix, Lancôme, Amazon, and department stores such as Macy's and Kolh's use this stratagem heavily in incentives. The five-dollar foot-long Subway sandwich was started by one failing franchisee in Miami. It not only rescued his own Subway franchise but also became a successful corporate marketing scheme. Consider these incentives:

- Bundle and package products together to create the perception of a bargain.

- Give away samples as bait, luring the customer in for a bigger purchase.

- To make the offer irresistible, include a gift with the purchase.

- To draw foot traffic to your store, sell a few items as loss leaders.

- Offer a free trial subscription to get the prospect hooked.

- Launch temporary "buy one, get one free," "buy two, get one free," "one-dollar item," or other forms of discount-on-volume promotion to increase sales volume.

Negotiation

The most common mistake by negotiators is to make concessions easily, thinking that the gestures will create goodwill, soften the other party, and win a deal. But it is more likely that concessions will make the other party greedy and suggest that you are in a weak position. If you must make a concession—"sacrifice the plum tree"—to win a deal ("preserve the peach tree"), remember:

- Get something for every concession you make.

- Make sure the other party values the concession you make.

- Make small concessions, and make them slowly.

- Never accept the first offer.

- Be patient even though it seems to take forever.

QUESTIONS TO CONSIDER

✓ *What are you willing to risk to achieve higher rewards?*

✓ *What should you be willing to sacrifice to strengthen your business position in the marketplace?*

✓ *How do you calculate your risk?*

Stratagem 12:
Steal a Goat Along the Way

Exploit your enemy's small lapses for your gain. Be alert, and turn opportunity to your advantage. Turn all your enemy's minuscule negligences to your benefit.

—The 36 Stratagems

LONG AGO IN CHINA

Liu Bang was a Han-dynasty warrior who later proclaimed himself the Han emperor during the Qin dynasty (221-206 B.C.). To consolidate his power in western China, he fought many wars, one of which was the prolonged fight against Xiang Yu, a prince of Western Chu. After trying and failing to assassinate Liu Bang at a banquet, Xiang Yu named Liu Bang the prince of Han and moved him to the land of Yizhou, meanwhile capturing his father and wife. While Liu Bang was sneaking through the Chen Cang passage to reenter China during the war against Xiang Yu, he discovered three territories under his enemy's control. Tucked into an out-of-the-way corner of China, these little states lay undefended. Liu took them over at once. This was unplanned, but the territories later proved to be of great strategic value.

MODERN APPLICATIONS

Vietnamese versus Indonesian Chicken Wings

In the process of expanding its franchises and licensing globally, Vietnam-based Pho 24 reaped great success but made a few blunders as well. Its Indonesian franchisees insisted on serving Indonesian-style chicken wings—a side dish popular with locals. But Ly, Pho 24's Vietnamese founder, insisted that Pho 24 was and must remain an authentic Vietnamese eatery brand. Refusing to compromise on its brand, yet reluctant to lose such a big customer base, Ly went back to his mom to find a solution. In their kitchen, they reexamined how the Vietnamese traditional chicken wings were prepared with fish sauce. By making certain changes with the fish sauce preparation, they came up with wings that would appeal to the Indonesian palate while remaining true to the standard of an authentic Vietnamese menu. The delectable concoction of the newfound Vietnamese-style chicken wing became an instant hit as a side dish at Pho 24 outlets in Indonesia. When I interviewed him, Ly said that with open mind we can turn a challenge into new possibilities.

Asian Car Manufacturers

From the late 1940s to the mid-1960s, U.S. automakers dominated the industry in their own domestic market and started to expand to Europe as well. But in the late 1970s and 1980s, while Japanese automakers such as Toyota and Honda tapped into the potential market in Asia, U.S. producers paid little attention, assuming that the markets were too small and the people too poor to afford big, expensive American cars. As a result, no U.S. automaker had a prominent presence in the market. Growing up in Vietnam during that time, I knew of Ford only through my mother's story of the old days. Then, in the 1990s, Korean automakers such as Hyundai joined the game and became popular.

Today, while the traditional markets in North America, Europe, and Japan are saturated, the emerging markets in Asia are growing fast. Globally the demand in well-developed markets of North America, Europe, and Japan is growing at only 2 percent annually. Asia has grown fast, becoming a hub of rapid development and expansion thanks to its rapidly emerging middle-class consumers. Japanese and Korean companies have established a strong presence and brand awareness in the region, and they have reaped tremendous rewards for their efforts. Meanwhile, American automakers struggle as late entrants with insignificant competitive advantages in a crowded marketplace.

Xerox

In the late 1990s, Xerox had a mountain of debt, and its share price had shrunk depressingly low thanks to fierce competition from Asian-made copiers and other hardware. Ursula Burns, the first African-American female CEO of a Fortune 500 company, made a huge and risky acquisition of $6.4 billion to turn Xerox around.

The goal was to make the company an instant player in the $500 billion market for technical business solutions. Her prudent vision did not come without fierce resistance. But the acquisition was the right strategy, and Xerox now draws 55 percent of its revenue from services, not hardware. It made a bold move by embracing disruptive forces, which helped it reset the playing field to its advantage.

Big Fish: A Student Start-up

When Kenny Nguyen and Gus Murillo attended a speech by a Fortune 500 company CEO on the Louisiana State University campus, they were not all that impressed or inspired, because the speaker read to his audience while showing them two hundred boring slides. This sparked the idea of creating presentations that tell stories and resonate emotionally with viewers instead of just presenting facts, figures, bullet points, and clip art. In 2011, the two college students launched Big Fish Presentations, a company providing sophisticated content design and presentation training at a starting price of $2,500. Their customers range from small businesses to *Fortune* 500 corporations such as Oracle and Mutual of Omaha. Revenue increased from $58,000 in 2011 to $225,000 in 2012. Their service offerings have grown to include consulting design, script writing, and video production services. Kenny Nguyen left school to dedicate his full time to serving as the company's CEO.

IMPLEMENTATION TACTICS

> *In battle, there are direct and indirect methods of*
> *attack, yet these two in combination give birth to a series*
> *of maneuvers. Have you exhausted the possibilities?*
>
> —Sun Tzu

This stratagem "Steal a goat along the way" advises being ever vigilant for emerging opportunities regardless of the circumstances. With creativity and the ability to seize the moment, you can gain the competitive edge while the competition suffers in crisis. The Chinese word "crisis" comprises two elements: "danger" and "opportunity." And indeed, every crisis contains within it both possibilities. It is your perspective that determines the outcome. Xerox embraced disruptive forces and reset the playing field to its advantage. Both Ly of Pho 24, and Nguyen and Murillo of Big Fish have turned challenges into possibilities. The U.S. automakers missed a tremendous opportunity to dominate the market in Asia, because they failed to look beyond the obvious advantage. Remember, even when things look dark, stay open:

- Be on constant lookout for new opportunities; be alert to every possibility.

- In times of crisis, pause to look at the bigger picture: find the opportunity hiding in plain sight.

- Keep your vision open so that off-target possibilities don't slip past your radar.

- Develop a prudent outlook, and look beyond the obvious advantage.

- Don't be too focused on one target; you might miss arising opportunities around you.

- Turn disruptive forces to your advantage.

- Turn your weaknesses into possibilities.

QUESTIONS TO CONSIDER

✓ *What does your competition ignore?*

✓ *What opportunities might your competition's inaction offer you?*

✓ *What action do you need to take, what sacrifice do you need to make, to seize those opportunities?*

✓ *How might crisis force a set of actions that would not occur in time of peace?*

CHAPTER 3

Attacking Strategems

Stratagem 13:
Hit the Grass to Startle the Snake

Before making the next move, ascertain the enemy's circumstances. Make sure you know his situation. Repeated surveillance is the best way to discover the hidden enemy.

—The 36 Stratagems

LONG AGO IN CHINA

One day, in the county of Jian-zhou, a man had lost a precious stone. The local magistrate, Chen, was called in to investigate. He questioned several people but got no result. So Magistrate Chen laid a trap for those he suspected.

"I know of a temple," he told them, "whose bell has great spiritual power. Since you wasted my time, we must employ the supernatural powers to quickly tell us the truth."

The magistrate had the bell brought to the courthouse and had the suspects brought in to proclaim their guilt or innocence. He explained that if an innocent man touched the bell, it would remain silent, but if a guilty man touched the bell, it would ring out. He had instructed one of his assistants to secretly smear ink on the bell after the curtains were closed.

After lighting incense and chanting prayers, the magistrate had curtains hung around the bell. He then told each suspect to place his hand under the curtain and touch the bell. As they withdrew their hands, Chen would examine them. Everyone's hand was stained except one man's. He then confessed to the theft. He had not touched the bell, for fear that it would ring.

MODERN APPLICATIONS

Lululemon Athletica: A Different Way of Selling Athletic Apparel

My husband's aunt, who lives in Birmingham, Alabama, excitedly told us to stop by Lululemon at the Summit Birmingham before visiting her at her house. I told her that we had Lululemon in Atlanta, where I live, but she insisted. The storefront caught my attention at once. A replica of the city's famous statue of Vulcan, standing in front with his spear, edged the store's logo. The Vulcan statue is an homage to the people, history, and cultural foundation of the city, which rose to prominence during the heyday of the U.S. steel industry.

Lululemon was founded in 1998 in Vancouver, British Columbia, by Dennis Wilson, who wanted yoga clothes that stretched and flexed with the various positions. He started making clothes in his basement and marketing them by approaching athletes and runners on the beach near his neighborhood. At night, he ran a yoga studio in that same basement. After the first few stores' success in Canada, Lululemon began expanding rapidly in both Canada and the United States during the recession of 2009. Sales have almost quadrupled from $353 million in 2009 to $1.36 billion in 2012, and its stock price has soared from $5 per share in 2009 to $70 per share as of May 2013. Its phenomenal annual growth of 48.9 percent is attributable to its prominent application of "Hit the grass to startle the snake."

Randall Shearin writes, in the May 2013 *Shopping Center Business* magazine, that Lululemon uses a different approach from most retailers for locating its stores. Most retailers find where other retailers are setting up shop; Lululemon looks at the areas where yoga, running, and a health-conscious lifestyle are popular. Then it uses "Hit the grass to startle the snake": it tests the market and builds a community by opening a showroom before it ever expands leases and builds out a store. When a showroom is open, the team focuses its efforts by spending time in the community, recruiting local ambassadors who are yoga instructors and athletes. The first time I heard of the Lululemon brand was when my yoga instructor invited me to one of the company's yoga events: Yoga under the Sky, where about a hundred of us practiced yoga at an outdoor pool on a moonlit night. Then I was intrigued to attend a yoga workshop on the second level of a Lululemon showroom in Buckhead, a high-income area. Lululemon expands into a full-fledged store only when the showroom attracts a certain level of engagement in the community.

In addition to the ambassador program that connects local running and yoga figures to the store, Lululemon ties its physical appearance into the local market. Every storefront tells a unique story about the local community. To achieve this goal could be exhausting and costly for the retailer, but the investment and effort have paid off. The Vulcan statue at the Summit Birmingham store in Alabama, for example, became a tourist attraction. By bringing traffic, it leads customers to the store and establishes effective brand positioning. And by "hitting the grass" first, the company has "startled the snake" (determined the degree of local interest) before committing to open a store.

Giant Retailers with the Local Touch

In 2001, on a trip in Europe, I noticed H&M, a cool, affordable clothing store. And yet, it barely existed in the States (just one store in Manhattan, New York City). The company has expanded globally by slowly, carefully rolling out to new regions and countries. It owes its success to its application of "Beat the grass to startle the snake." In 2010, H&M rolled out many stores across the United States by testing its U.S. market through the New

York flagship store. I recall how excited my colleagues and I were to visit the first H&M in Atlanta, Georgia, when it opened near downtown. The unique element that sets H&M apart is that each store brings a particular local trend and flavor. It tracks local buying preferences, then stocks its inventory accordingly. When it develops the right mix, it moves fast to expand. Now H&M exists in forty-three countries and is ranked the second-largest global clothing retailer, just behind Zara and just ahead of GAP, the third-largest global clothing retailer.

Whole Foods, an international grocery chain with a local touch, has adopted the same strategy. Before opening at a location, it carefully tracks local buying habits. When I go to Whole Foods, I feel at home, and I'm happy to support the store when I see a sign telling me it has sourced local products: freshwater shrimp from local Georgia farms, handpicked peaches from a nearby orchard, free-range pork from Thompson Farms in Dixie, Georgia, or key lime pie from a local bakery. By launching small attacks, Whole Foods learns how the market reacts; then it launches the full attack to satisfy customers' wants and needs.

Starbucks Gets Back to Its Roots

Starbuck was rolling out too rapidly, losing the laid-back "Seattle coffeehouse" personal touch that it began with, and the European-style ambience that it endeavored to create. Seemingly overnight, I began to see Starbucks stores pop up like mushrooms, in grocery and retail chains such as Kroger and Target, and on every other street corner around my neighborhood. When I go grocery shopping, I see Starbucks coffee all over the shelves. By that point, the company was cannibalizing its own business. Fortunately for it, in early 2008, Howard Schultz returned to the CEO position to rescue Starbucks from the crisis. Noticing that the company had expanded too fast while ignoring the core competence that made it successful in the first place, Schultz closed six hundred stores so that his people could refocus and get back to what mattered most.

In *Onward: How Starbucks Fought for Its Life without Losing*

Its Soul, he writes, "We were closing almost 20 percent of our newest stores. We thought all we had to do was show up to be successful . . . A lesson resonated. The only number that mattered is 'one': One cup. One customer. One partner. One experience at a time. We had to get back to what mattered most."

If Starbucks had "beaten the grass" first before rolling out in every direction and neighborhood, it could have avoided a potentially disastrous misstep.

IMPLEMENTATION TACTICS

The stratagem "Beat the grass to startle the snake" suggests, instead of committing to a full-frontal assault, making a series of small attacks to gather information about your enemy and then responding accordingly. Lululemon, H&M, and Whole Foods are apt illustrations of taking small steps to guarantee success in every local business. Starbucks' misstep in the mid-2000s is a cautionary tale for businesses that roll out too fast without testing and adapting to the local market. So keep these points in mind:

- Launch a small-scale attack before committing to a full-scale plan.

- Launch a false attack so that your opponent reveals his real strengths or strategies.

- Test-market your product on a small scale to observe the market's reaction before committing major resources to launch the product.

This stratagem is also used in testing the reaction of your partner, counterpart, or any other potential business relationship. Coca-Cola acquired shares in Green Mountain Coffee to understand the coffee business and explore the opportunity to take over the company. Pepsi seized the opportunity by acquiring a sizable stake at brand O.N.E, to instantly take over a share of the coconut-water market, while Coca-Cola acquired Zico for the same reason. Google acquired a stake in its competitor Baidu China but, having "beaten the grass," did not like the signs, and it withdrew in 2005. You, too, should try it and see where the snakes pop up:

- Acquire a stake in a potential merger or acquisition target to feel out the market reaction before committing major resources.

- Suggest to potential counterparts, partners, and suppliers that you are looking at other opportunities, and watch how they react. Adjust your price, attitude, and behavior and revise terms/contracts to your advantage.

QUESTIONS TO CONSIDER

✓ *How often do you review your strategy to see what adjustments are needed?*

✓ *What is your plan to test the waters before you make the next big commitment?*

✓ *How are you going to test your customers' loyalty before you must depend on it when instituting a major change?*

Stratagem 14:
Borrow a Corpse to Resurrect a Soul

*Since the weak needs help, he is easier to approach
than the powerful. Exploit and manipulate the weak,
for you give him your strength at his request.*

—The 36 Stratagems

LONG AGO IN CHINA

During the Spring and Autumn period, separate states all over China fought one another for dominion. Qin defeated and annexed the other states, including Chu, which covered the largest territory of all. There were rebellions and uprisings. Among these was the uncle-nephew team of Xiang Liang and Xiang Yu, who rebelled against the Qin empire to reclaim their home state of Chu.

Xiang Liang was advised to find a direct descendent of the former Chu king. Although the descendant would not be an immediate member of the Xiang family, because of his royal lineage he would exert influence, ignite patriotism, and invoke the spirit of the Chu people.

So Xiang Liang launched a search until he found a grandson of the former Chu king—a poor shepherd. The shepherd agreed to become king and adopted his grandfather's name. The crowning of the new king of Chu marked a pivotal moment for the Chu state and gave impetus to the rebellion against the Qin empire.

MODERN APPLICATIONS

Yum! Brands Resurrects Its Soul in Asia

After delivering a seminar in Beijing, I took a quick walk from the Hilton Hotel to Pizza Hut, expecting to get a slice of pizza fast so that we could go back to our hotel room and catch up with work. Surprisingly, I was greeted by a nicely dressed hostess who signaled us to wait in the waiting room. Twenty-five minutes later, I was ushered upstairs to an immaculate, stylish dining area the equal of any well-appointed, jam-packed fusion restaurant in San Francisco. The menu had appetizers including chicken wings, fried squid, and delectable rice dishes, and pizza choices customized for local tastes, such as a seafood pizza topped with prawns and crab sticks. (In East Asia, seafoods and snails are considered a rare delicacy, and the entrées are elaborate, ranging from salmon rolls to lobster, to escargot in garlic oil.)

Yum! Brands uses the same strategy for its KFC stores in Asia. It adopts the best of U.S. fast-food concepts and tweaks them to cater to the palates and dining habits of Asian customers. I invited an old friend and her family to a dinner in Ho Chi Minh City, Vietnam. When asked which restaurant they wanted, they said in an excited chorus, "KFC!" I politely said I would like to treat them to a nicer place. But they insisted, and I had a chance to experience a complete resurrection of KFC's brand in this part of the world. Surrounded by young middle-class diners in an upbeat modern ambience, I could not imagine this same name being associated with a no-frills, low-priced fast-food chain in the United States.

Pizza Hut and KFC (food chains under Yum! Brands) have successfully reinvented and positioned themselves as a delicious, fast-paced, modern-lifestyle choice in Asia, where customers still have very deeply rooted culinary tastes yet are looking for the trappings of modern Western style. By "borrowing a corpse," Yum! Brands has "resurrected a soul" to fit the new Asia. As a result, the food chain has enjoyed phenomenal success. China alone accounted for more than 40 percent of Yum! Brands' 2012 global revenue.

Asia's continued fast growth presents tremendous opportunities. There will be over three billion new middle-class consumers in 2030—five times the number in Europe and ten times those in North America.

Other Businesses: "Never Give Up"

Failing businesses can restructure or file for Chapter 11 bankruptcy protection to reorganize while getting a breath of new life at the same. Companies can also change their name or create joint ventures with a new partner to repurpose themselves.

Over the years, training companies have tended to use the same core material—revised and updated but not substantially changed. But changing the title of a course to embrace new trends and buzzwords in the industry is vital for training and business development. For example, what were known as "problem-solving skills" became "critical-thinking skills." The past five years have seen a new trend toward "leadership," with not so much about "management" anymore. While there are some distinctions between "leadership" and "management" principles, there is enormous overlap and similarity.

Developing commercial real estate could feel like putting moving pieces of puzzles together. A developer looks for the right piece of dirt, works with a big chain such as Home Depot, Walmart, or Kroger to secure an anchor, and has the makings of a shopping center. First, he needs to secure the land. Then he invests money in getting some groundwork done while waiting for a big-box company to go through committee after committee for approval. It could take three years for a deal to get rejected or approved. It's a long process. When the economy doesn't boom, the process languishes even longer, and the rejection rate goes up. At one point, David, a broker turned developer, saw his business undergoing a slow death. Refusing to "die," he changed tactics, especially during the recent economic downturn. He raises capital, buys a distressed or nonperforming shopping center at a bargain, and revives it with cosmetic improvement, new management, and new tenants. He can either choose to own and manage the property or turn it around and sell it. From humble beginnings, David has amassed a net worth of over $45 million. While conventional thinking advises dumping a nonperforming property, he collects these "corpses" and "resurrects a soul."

Água de Coco: *Old Idea, New Branding*

A conversation with two young Brazilian women ignited a great business idea for Ira Liran and Michael Kirban. When asked what they missed most about their country, one of the young women answered, "*Água de coco.*" Two months later in Brazil, visiting one of the Brazilian women (who would become his wife), Liran started researching the prospect of branding coconut water for the American market. After several months working with coconut plantations and producers, making connections, and learning the business culture in Brazil, Vita Coco was born.

Meanwhile, Kirban started the initial market research in New York, meeting with potential beverage distributors and building awareness of coconut water. In 2004, they brought Vita Coco to market in a few stores along the East Coast. Pitching to celebrities to be their company's investors and endorse the product was an effective strategy in bringing natural coconut water to American consumers accustomed to sugary carbonated beverages. The brand initially drew attention in the U.S. market after Madonna, along with a few other Hollywood celebrities, invested in the company. Vita Coco became the number oneselling U.S. coconut-water brand, with 2012 revenue of $150 million.

Coconut water is chipping away at the $100-billion market for nonalcoholic beverages. The beverage industry is looking for the next big thing as the health-consciousness movement makes soda sales flat and shrinking. Coca-Cola planned to exercise its option to acquire a majority stake in Zico, the number two U.S. coconut-water brand by sales. In 2010, Pepsi acquired a majority stake in O.N.E., the number three U.S. coconut-water brand. Pepsi also has its own line of coconut water in the Naked Juice line. With U.S. soda sales in decline for more than half a decade, giant beverage companies increasingly acquire stakes in emerging brands and new-drink categories. By adopting the drinking habits of the Brazilians, Liran and Kirban have created a new drink category for the U.S. market.

Mamma Mia!: *Global Smash Hit*

I recall the first time I heard ABBA's music in the early 1980s. Along with Vietnamese pop songs, every street and alleyway in Saigon was filled with the strains of the Swedish group's music. Learning to play guitar, I started my lessons with songs by ABBA, including "I Have a Dream," "Chiquitita," "Fernando," and "The Winner Takes It All." During 197282, ABBA was one of the hugest international pop groups of all time, topping the charts again and again in Europe, North America, Latin America, and Australia. And yet, the band dissolved in late 1982, and its music was gradually washed away by new music genres and emerging bands. Almost two decades had gone by when, on a trip to Europe in 2001, I found out, to my complete astonishment, that British Broadway had resurrected ABBA's music by creating *Mamma Mia!*— a stage musical based on the group's songs. Ever since, *Mamma Mia!* has played in more than forty countries on five continents. The smash success led to the *Mamma Mia!* movie adaptation. Just one year after its 2008 release, the movie, produced with a budget of $52 million, had grossed a worldwide total of over $600 million, becoming one of the largest-grossing musical movies ever made.

IMPLEMENTATION TACTICS

The stratagem "Borrow a Corpse to Resurrect a Soul" comes from the Chinese belief that the dead can be reincarnated. It is believed that when you are dead, your corpse is rotten but your soul is still alive. In order to be propped up and rise again as a new human being, the soul needs a "corpse." In life, when you face a setback or defeat, you must never give up your "soul." As long as your soul is strong and alive, you will find a "corpse"—something that your competition has abandoned—in which to return to life and strike back. David, the shopping center developer, is a good illustration. In the economy's downturn, his development business was dead. But his strong will (the "soul") has found new a "corpse"—distressed properties that his competition isn't interested in. As a result, his business revives and thrives in the new "corpse."

The stratagem also suggests reviving the "dead," old, forgotten idea. Since it has been abandoned by the competition, now it can become your unique competitive edge. Yum! Brands revived the fading low-end fast-food concept into a hip, new, successful concept in Asia. Coconut water, a popular drink in Brazil and Asia, was infused with a new healthy-drink purpose and introduced to the U.S. market. The forgotten, "dead" ABBA songs were picked up to make a smash musical play and, later, the blockbuster movie *Mamma Mia!* Sometimes, you don't need to innovate—just revive a forgotten idea to gain a competitive advantage. What "corpse" can you borrow and breathe new life into?

- Revive old ideas by infusing them with a new purpose.

- Merge, acquire, buy in, or buy them out when a business has the potential and is not too expensive to acquire.

- Liquidate or restructure a failing business or organization to reposition it in a new light.

- Test different names or purposes with the same content to see which one works best or how the market responds to it.

- Reinvent or rebrand by building on existing ideas.

- Adopt and adapt an idea to fit the market.

QUESTIONS TO CONSIDER

✓ *What do you notice that has been forgotten but still has the glint of gold?*

✓ *What abandoned asset has good value if you only repurpose or rebrand it?*

✓ *What are the risks and potential rewards if you should do so?*

✓ *How do you "resurrect," or leverage, its forgotten value?*

✓ *What action do you take to "resurrect" it most efficiently and effectively?*

Stratagem 15:
Lure the Tiger from its Mountain Lair

Use unfavorable natural conditions to trap your enemy. Create deception to lure him out. In an attack that involves great risk, draw your enemy out of his comfort zone; then destroy him.

—The 36 Stratagems

LONG AGO IN CHINA

By the end of the Han dynasty (221 B.C.-A.D. 220), China's warlords had consolidated power into a few states. Among them were two great rivals, Sun Ce and Liu Xun. Liu Xun's city was well fortified and surrounded by mountains, making it nearly impossible to attack. Sun Ce, on the other hand, ruled a much smaller state and had little hope of conquering Liu Xun.

One day, Sun Ce sent an ambassador bearing gifts and a humble letter to Liu Xun. Liu Xun was pleased by the gesture and the words of self-abasement from Sun Ce. In the letter, Sun Ce also mentioned another state, Shangliao, which regularly attacked his territory. He proposed that Liu Xun attack Shangliao, using Sun Ce's reinforcements. Sun Ce enumerated all the benefits that the victory would bring to Liu Xin: territorial expansion, wealth from the rich state of Shangliao, and even greater power.

Liu Xun's adviser argued that he did not trust Sun Ce, and pointed out that if Sun Ce failed to provide reinforcements, his army would be depleted. He further warned that if Liu Xun left his mountain stronghold with his best soldiers, the remaining army's strength would be impaired, and his base would be easily attacked by Sun Ce while he was away on this quest against Shangliao.

But Liu Xun, ever greedy for more wealth and power, ignored his adviser's words. His army marched to Shangliao and surrounded the city. Unprepared for the fierce battle and exhausted from travel, their only hope was the reinforcements from Sun Ce. But these never came. Meanwhile, Sun Ce ordered his troops to attack Liu Xun's city, which was vulnerable now with its best men absent.

Liu Xun and his army were defeated at Shangliao. Disheartened, they returned only to find their home conquered by Sun Ce. After some futile last efforts, they surrendered to Sun Ce.

MODERN APPLICATIONS

Negotiate on Your Home Turf

As we discussed when studying stratagem 4, Asian businesses tend to invite Western businesses over to their home turf for negotiations. This gives them home-court advantage. Also, businesspeople traveling from the West can be exhausted from prolonged travel, a new environment, and the effort to comprehend the local language and customs. Being away from headquarters and their best team of advisers, they can let their guard down. Thus handicapped, they are not in the best position to make smart decisions. The counterpart takes advantage of this by maneuvering the negotiation his way and asking for more concessions and more favorable terms.

Zara Clones the Tiger

Zara, the company that introduced the fast-fashion trend, is based in Arteixo, a small town in northwestern Spain. Speed and responsiveness sets Zara apart from other big fashion retailers.

For Zara to achieve that speed, it must have a competitive edge: its supply chain. Design, manufacturing, and distribution channels are highly centralized. About half Zara's clothes are made in Spain or nearby countries. Susan Berfield and Manuel Baigorri note in *Bloomberg Businessweek*'s January 2, 2014, issue that Zara owes its success to centralization. In 2013, China surpassed France to become Zara's second-largest marketplace in numbers of stores. This remote market presents challenges to the supply chain of a company whose success depends on centralization. Even though Zara is expanding globally, it does not allow its core competency to weaken. As soon as it decided to go global, the company knew it must have two systems of centralization: one in Spain and one in China. Zara in China is a different Zara, customized for China and nearby markets. The tiger that is Zara does not let itself be lured from the mountain. On the contrary, it replicates its success by cloning itself—creating a second "tiger" for China.

Pixar versus Disney

The films *Toy Story* and *Cars,* as well as many Star Trek sequences, are but a few of the Pixar team's computer-animated masterpieces. In 1986, right after leaving Apple, Steve Jobs bought Pixar for $10 million. The company avoided head-on competition with Disney by producing films that used digital animation experts rather than actors (except for the voices).Pixar partnered with Disney for several years, and both companies benefited from the synergistic arrangement: Pixar owned the creativity team; Disney had the powerful distribution channels. But the relationship deteriorated because Steve Jobs refused to make movies by Hollywood's hidebound rules. The powerful "tiger" Disney was "lured from its mountain lair" when it tried to compete with Pixar in producing computer-animated movies. But its stronghold was weakened because Disney could not match Pixar's digital-animation expertise and capacities. Disney stopped trying and ended up acquiring Pixar for $7.4 billion in 2006.

IMPLEMENTATION TACTICS

*In war, do not repeat the tactics that have gained
you one victory. Rather, let your methods be
determined by the infinite variety of circumstances.*

—Sun Tzu

The idea for this stratagem is that hunting a ferocious tiger is difficult and dangerous—all the more so if the tiger is in its home terrain. But lure it out of its mountain stronghold and into the city, and it is at a serious disadvantage. By removing your enemy's advantage and putting its stronghold at risk, you have a better chance to win. Zara, in the role of the tiger, refused to dilute its core strength of centralization. Instead, it cloned itself to produce another "tiger," this one indigenous to the Asian terrain. Disney, on the other hand, failing to match Pixar's digital animation capabilities, was obliged to acquire it at a premium price.

Some key elements to remember:

- Impair or nullify your opponent's strengths by luring him out of his comfort zone or stronghold.

- Focus on your core competency, and keep improving what you are best at.

- Weaken your opponent or counterpart by luring him away from his support system, onto your turf.

- Avoid competing head-on with your enemy at what he is best at. Instead, reverse the situation and make him compete in what *you* are best at.

- Influence others' decision making by drawing them away from their norms, routines, and comfort zones. When you do, emotions are more easily tapped, and critical thinking is weakened, leaving them vulnerable.

- Find a "territory" (market segment, product, service) where no tigers are operating; thus, you don't need to exert resources to lure them out.

- If you need to lure a tiger out, use bait, instill fear, feign an attack on its territory, or provoke it.

QUESTIONS TO CONSIDER

✓ *What is your competition's stronghold?*

✓ *How do you entice your competition out of its comfort zone?*

✓ *How do you disrupt your competition's routines?*

✓ *How can you maneuver your competition away from its support system?*

Stratagem 16:
Release the Enemy to Recapture Him

Drive the enemy into a corner, and he may retaliate fiercely. Do not destroy him, but let him go, and his morale will falter. Tire him out, and his fighting spirit will waver. Then you will be able to capture him without bloodshed. Once your enemy does not believe he can win, it is time to claim victory.

—The 36 Stratagems

LONG AGO IN CHINA

During the time of the Three Kingdoms, Zhu Ge Liang, the prime minister of Shu, was the renowned master of the art of war. He battled against eastern, northern, and southern tribal rivals.

Menguo, king of the southern tribes, gathered the leaders of the Three Gorges and declared that they must unite to resist the powerful Shu.

But Menguo and his army were no match for Zhu Ge Liang's masterful strategies and skilled fighters, and he and his troops were defeated and captured in the first battle. Zhu Ge Liang treated Menguo and his men well with food and wine and eventually let them go. They returned and attacked Shu again the following day, and again they were captured. Even though a prisoner, Menguo declared to Zhu Ge Liang that he refused to yield and that he would gather his forces to fight again. Zhu Ge Liang knew that Menguo was a righteous man; thus, Zhu Ge Liang was better off winning his heart than counting victories. So when Menguo said that he would not yield, especially to a Chinese ruler, Zhu let him go again.

After being released the second time, Menguo allied himself with Wutugu, another powerful tribal leader. By now, Menguo had been in and out of Zhu Ge Liang's camp twice, and he felt that Zhu Ge Liang had run out of strategies. Thus, Menguo was confident that this time, he would win. He hastened down the valley in triumph, only to find that Wutugu and his army had been ambushed and wiped out by Zhu Ge Liang. Menguo and his family members were captured but were taken to a tent and served food and wine. During the meal, Zhu Ge Liang's messenger said, "Zhu Ge Liang has commissioned me to release you. Mobilize another force against him if you can, and try one more time if you think you can defeat him. Now, go!" But this time, Menguo wept. "Nothing like this has ever happened," he said. "Though I do not share your culture and your ways, I do not lack a sense of what is right. O great Minister, yours is the majesty of heaven. We men of the South will never again resist your rule."

MODERN APPLICATIONS

Hot-Dog Stand Uses the Honor System

Amin is a veteran who started a hot-dog business on New York City's Fifth Avenue. Every day, his stand is packed with routine customers as well as tourists. Among the thousands of hot-dog vendors hustling on the busy streets, he is the one who makes the news. Having paid a high price for his spot, Amin didn't have much financial room to hire more help. As a result, he watched in frustration as customers queued up in long lines and ended up leaving in droves due to the long wait. To solve the issue, Amin uses the "release the enemy to recapture him" stratagem. Realizing that the bottleneck occurred when he had to stop preparing the food to receive money and dig through his bucket to seek change for a customer, he tackled the bottleneck. He puts a basket out at the end of the stand with a note that says, "Thank you!" A customer steps up, waits for a few seconds to pick up the hot dog and drink, steps to the end of the stand, and leaves money in the basket. The basket not only frees him up from the most time-consuming task in the whole hot-dog selling sequence, but strikes a chord with customers—and with national news. When asked if people ever cheat, he smiled and said, "I don't know. I just know I make more money than I did before. I'm happy when return customers support me and want me to do well in this very unstable hot-dog business." By "releasing" the customers—allowing them to pay on the honor system—Amin "captures" even more customers thanks to a lean operation and "recaptures" loyal and supportive ones.

The Return of the Viet Kieu

Being born and raised in Vietnam, I saw firsthand how this stratagem was adopted, both ineffectively and effectively. After the fall of Saigon in 1975, the North Vietnamese army took over the South and united the country. Strongly influenced by Chinese culture and thought processes, the new government had done many things to eradicate the old Southern elites and intellectuals. It was similar to the Cultural Revolution in China, though to a much lesser extent. My stepfather and uncles were put in reeducation camps for over ten years because they had fought for the South Vietnamese. The result was an exodus of rich, well-educated Southerners. These so-called boat people would rather put their lives at the mercy of the ocean than continue living in their own home country. My mother twice put me on a fishing boat to cross the ocean, when I was 10 and 11, but I was arrested at the border right before the boat departed for Thailand, where there were refugee camps.

In 1986, Vietnam implemented its first set of liberalization policies, or *doi moi* (renovation). These *doi moi* reforms shifted Vietnam's Soviet-style centrally planned economy at the end of the Vietnam War (1975) toward economic liberalization—especially those reforms that focused on foreign trade and investment and promoted a higher level of international economic integration. But for almost twenty years, the Vietnamese diaspora, or Viet

Kieu, especially those residing in the United States, had a hard time returning Vietnam, thanks to the U.S. trade embargo, which did not end until February 1994.

In May 2004, Resolution 36/NQ-TW of the Politburo on overseas Vietnamese affairs was passed with the purpose of offering support to Viet Kieu and recognizing the Viet Kieu community and their potential for making a significant contribution to Vietnam's economy. Now Viet Kieu are welcome back home to work, reunite with family, and contribute to building the country. The government has made it easy for them to return to their own country, by instituting loosened investment regulation, favorable immigration policy, and more liberal and transparent economic policies. As a result, Vietnam has an influx of people returning there from all over the world. Many of these returnees have the skills, expertise, and capital to contribute greatly to the country's economic development and prosperity.

Luring Talent

In 2001, I had a chance to visit the state-of-the-art Microsoft campus where my friend Hiep, a Harvard graduate, worked. It was an amazing place that offered a twenty-four-hour five-star buffet, a gym, sleeping corners, showers, a massage studio, and day care. The benefits and convenience attracted loads of talent. It was a place where they could work, make friends, socialize, eat, and hang out. As a result, they could spend more time on projects, discussing project ideas, networking, and building relationships. This all contributed to making Microsoft a better company both culturally and financially. The Google campus in Palo Alto, California, used this model later on and, arguably, to an even greater extent. Those Microsoft and Google campuses are adaptations of "Release the enemy to recapture him." By giving the people more freedom and perks at camp, those young talents ended up spending more time at work and contributing more to the company.

Singapore, Malaysia, Taiwan, and Hong Kong are good at

attracting offshore wealth and foreign professionals to settle there. By providing liberal investment and immigration policies, creating attractive living conditions and infrastructure, offering favorable rentals for expatriate professionals, and relaxing the tax system, they make their countries more attractive than the expatriates' own home countries. Singapore, in particular, has encouraged foreigners to acquire Singaporean citizenship—thus obtaining the new citizens' *full* commitment. The Taiwanese government offered attractive packages to lure Taiwanese and Chinese scientists and researchers in California's Silicon Valley to work for Taiwan's Science Park. Korea caught on and began wooing Japanese quality engineers and scientists, offering them high salaries and perks to work for Korean companies in both Korea and Japan.

IMPLEMENTATION TACTICS

An army suffers from flight, rebellion, collapse, ruin, disorder, and rout. These six calamities are not attributable to natural causes. They are the fault of the general.

—Sun Tzu

This stratagem advises capturing an enemy without bloodshed. On the contrary, wear down his fighting spirit, and he will give in voluntarily. In business, to secure complete surrender and loyalty, you need to win the other's heart and mind.

Sales and Marketing

- Don't try to sell. Build relationships first.
- Don't push a product. Build a community around it.
- Don't sell products on price. Add value.
- Don't start a sales pitch. Ask questions and listen "actively."

Leadership and Management

- Don't motivate by relying solely on extrinsic rewards. Build a culture.

- Be patient to earn trust and credibility. It pays off handsomely.

- Motivate people through winning their hearts and minds.

- Don't micromanage. Lead by delegating and empowering.

We sometimes assume that we must dominate and destroy our competition. "Release the enemy to recapture him" advises that the most important thing is to *understand the situation*. Sometimes our success depends on our competition's continued existence and success.

- Cooperate with your competition to gain synergy.

- Learn to coexist with your competition, and break free when you have gained enough strength.

QUESTIONS TO CONSIDER

✓ *What can you do to build strong relationships with customers, providers, and employees?*

✓ *How can you build a company culture that encourages individuals to excel?*

✓ *What motivates the people in your business? What motivates people to do business with you?*

✓ *How can you join forces with your competition to influence the industry, regulation, and government?*

Stratagem 17:
Toss Out a Brick to Get a Jade

Use a bait to entice the enemy. Get his mind
muddled, and he will fall into the trap.

—The 36 Stratagems

LONG AGO IN CHINA

Marquis Jing, the most powerful of the six nobles in the kingdom of Jin in the mid-fifth century B.C., demanded a piece of land from the state of Wei. The prince of Wei refused. Then his adviser said, "If you give him the piece of land now, his greed and arrogance will grow, and he will demand more land from other neighboring states. At that point, the neighboring states will join forces against him, for he becomes a threat to all."

The prince of Wei followed this advice and gave Marquis Jing a fiefdom of ten thousand households. As expected, Marquis Jing was encouraged by this, and he soon asked for more from the neighboring state of Zhao. When rejected, Marquis Jing mounted an attack against Zhao. The neighboring States of Han and Wei, anticipating that it would soon be their turn to receive demands for more fiefdoms, hurried to provide enforcements to assist Zhao. Unable to fight against the joined forces, Marquis Jing lost his life.

Wei gave away the "brick" of a fiefdom to get a "jade"—the destruction of the powerful Marquis Jing of Jin.

MODERN APPLICATIONS

Our neighborhood was thrilled when the dollar-theater company Picture Show took over the failing first-run theater ten years ago. I can take my boys and their friends to a movie and pay as little as a dollar per ticket. I can entertain the kids without paying full price to see a first-run film. These dollar theaters target teenagers, youth groups, retirees, large families with many children, and adults who missed a movie's first release. They treat second-run films as loss leaders—the "brick"—by charging little for admission, in an effort to make bigger profits on high-markup concession items and activities such as school get-togethers, babysitting service, and birthday parties (the "jade").

Amazon signs a lot of book deals and sells the books at cost—or even at a loss—to create customer loyalty. It then sells e-books for free or from $0.99 up to $2.99 to lure customers into buying its Kindle reader. The Kindle is also provided at a low price, because Amazon plans to make its money on sales of a variety of e-books. Today, a Kindle app is downloaded free on any "smart" electronic device. Amazon figures it can sell even more e-books through its free Kindle app on competitors' devices. Amazon's profit is less than 2 percent, or at the break-even point, but its stock price keeps rising because of the tremendous market share it accumulates by using "Toss out a brick to get a jade" many times over.

When the iPhone 5 was released around June 2012, it was worth about $850. Verizon captured the mobile phone service by offering the iPhone 5 for $125 with a two-year contract commitment.

Gas stations sell gas at break-even or a marginal profit to lure drivers to their convenience stores, where they make a hefty profit on snacks, cigarettes, soft drinks, sunglasses, and on-the-go food.

Car manufacturers can make marginal profits or even barely break even on selling cars, but make handsome profits on parts and service.

Deere & Company provides equipment, including tractors and engines, as well as tools, technology, and services to construction, forestry, and landscaping users. The company makes 6 percent profit on hardware, 25 percent on parts, 31 percent on service, and much more on technology.

Developing countries with open-door policies and favorable investment regulations attract foreign investment from countries such as China, Vietnam, and Malaysia. In return, the country benefits from transferred technology, skill development, and job creation. On the other hand, foreign enterprises benefit from an existing distribution network, established contacts and connections, low labor costs, and tax avoidance in their own countries.

IMPLEMENTATION TACTICS

Thus, one who is skillful at keeping his enemy on the move, and maintaining deceitful appearances on which the enemy will act, sacrifices something that the enemy may snatch at it. By holding out baits, he keeps the enemy on the march. Then, with a body of handpicked men, he lies in wait for him.

—Sun Tzu

The literal translation of "Toss out a brick to get a jade" simply means trading something of lower value for something of higher value. However, while it sounds simplistic, the meaning can be deeper. According to Lao Tzu's philosophy, there is never an absolute value for anything. Long and short form each other; beautiful and ugly complement each other; being and nonbeing give birth to each other. In other words, value depends on what one plans to do with the item or resource in question. The key to success is in identifying what another values and creating an opportunity for exchange.

Key elements to remember:

- In negotiations or marketing, give away something you value in order to trade for what you value more. Concede something that is less important to you but more important to your counterpart.

- Avoid treating your product/service as a commodity. Add value and turn it into a consultative sale at a premium price.

- Identify the difference between what you value and what others value to create possibilities for you to exchange profitably.

- Define your value. Value is relative. What is of great value to you may be of little or no value to others, and vice versa.

- Create and add value. Don't let others dictate your value.

QUESTIONS TO CONSIDER

✓ *What can you provide to a prospect or client that would yield more business for them?*

✓ *What can you provide to a prospect or client that would yield more business for you?*

✓ *How will you add value to your product or service to separate yourself from the competition?*

✓ *What questions can you ask to get a better understanding of your prospect's or client's needs and wants?*

Stratagem 18:
Disband the Enemy by Neutralizing its Leader

Capture his leader and your enemy's strength will break down. His situation is as dire as that of a sea dragon fighting on land.

—The 36 Stratagems

LONG AGO IN CHINA

In A.D. 757, the emperor of the Tang Dynasty commanded General Zhang Xun to guard his city from the rebels, whose leader was General Yin Zi Qi. Zhang Xun's army had bravely attacked the opposing army and killed five thousand enemy troops. Victory was not yet declared, because, amid the confusion, no one could identify General Yin Zi Qi.

General Zhang Xun ordered his men to shoot off arrows made of rue branches and straw. Seeing this, the opposing soldiers were delighted, assuming that Zhang Xun's soldiers had run out of arrows and were reduced to shooting such useless missiles. They rushed gleefully to report the good news to their leader. Thus, they not only helped Zhang Xun identify who Yin Zi Qi was, but they also revealed his hideout. Zhang Xun ordered his troops to shoot real arrows at the rebel general. An arrow hit him in the left eye, and he withdrew from the battle. Though he managed to escape, his troops were defeated utterly.

MODERN APPLICATIONS

Hunting the Leader at a Class Reunion

In a class reunion party in 2010, I got to see most of my high school friends. As in any class reunion, we noticed that some had become professionally and financially successful; others, not so much. Lena had always been one of the brightest students in every subject, to say nothing of her impeccable communication skills and outgoing personality. She is now vice president of a Swiss aroma-and-flavoring company that has established a solid business-to-business customer base in Vietnam, including with Nestle, Unilever, and many other major players that joined the market since the United States lifted the embargo in 1997. Another successful figure is Phan, who was not all that "book smart" but had the moxie and chutzpah of a serial entrepreneur. And indeed, he is a self-made multimillionaire who owns four enterprises, one of which is the aroma-and-flavor cash cow. In the bustling atmosphere of the reunion, Phan's wife did not forget to "romance" Lena to work for her and her husband. If Lena agrees, not only will she be an amazing leader and contributor, but, most importantly, she will open up a new network and high-caliber customer base for Phan's business. A savvy businessman never stops hunting for a "qualified leader." For Sun Tzu says, a leader determines whether the nation (business) shall be in power (growth) or peril.

How Google Captures Leading Talents

Google established a strategic recruiting office in Kirkland, Washington, a five-minute drive from Microsoft headquarters, to recruit talent from Microsoft. On the site, it offered a lot of perks and generous benefits to lure candidates to sign the employment contract on the spot. They did so knowing that when project leaders leave an organization, they tend to take with them talented and trusted people who work well with them. In China, Google stations itself strategically between Beijing University and Tsinghua University, where it aims at tapping the top Chinese engineering graduate students.

Dr. Kai Fu Lee, a Carnegie Mellon University PhD, started working for Microsoft China in 1998 and founded Microsoft Research Asia, a top-flight research lab in Beijing. In 2000, he was transferred to Microsoft's U.S. headquarters to oversee the company's strategy in research and to develop strategies for China. Lee was handsomely compensated for his work, making $1 million in 2004 alone.

In spring 2005, Google planned to open a major research operation in China and offered to make Lee president of its new China operations if he would leave Microsoft. Even with all the contractual complications that had to be sorted through, Lee decided to leave Microsoft for Google. He was a celebrated computer scientist who had worked for Apple before Microsoft. In the book *In the Plex,* Steven Levy says that Lee toured the country like a rock star, recruiting talents and speaking on Google's behalf. He had thousands of engineering students following him on his Web site and seeking his advice. In addition to attracting engineers in droves, Lee also took with him key employees who had worked for him at Microsoft.

Marissa Mayer, Superwoman of the New Yahoo

In the summer of 2012, Yahoo hired Marissa Mayer, a Google senior executive with thirteen years' experience, and named her CEO of its $5 billion revenue, $18 billion market capital, 700 millionuser company. A pay package valued at $36.6 million in salary and stock for 2012 alone shows that the board believes that she will transform Yahoo, which has had a rough past decade of failed product strategies, top talents lost to competitors, and failing leadership. According to Brad Stone (*Bloomberg Businessweek,* August 2013), despite an uphill battle and some stumbles, Yahoo's stock is up 75 percent since Mayer took over. "Marissa has done two things at Yahoo," says Ben Ling, a partner at venture capital firm Khosla Ventures and a former Google colleague. "She has made it an attractive place for top talent to work, and she has begun to release products that engage consumers on a daily basis."

Mayer has established a rescue team, spending nearly $200 million to acquire at least eighteen start-ups, picking up the blogging network Tumblr for $1.1 billion, hiring more mobile developers, and locking engineers into two- to four-year contracts and setting them loose to build apps. Mayer has the charisma, public image, credibility, and influence to breathe new life into Yahoo. By capturing one of Google's top executives, Yahoo could create a buzz and reclaim some lost market share.

IMPLEMENTATION TACTICS

The leader of armies is the decider of the people's fate, the man who determines whether the nation shall be in power or in peril.

—Sun Tzu

This stratagem advises capturing the enemy's leader as one of the most effective attacking stratagems. Without a leader, the enemy troops will quickly fall into disarray. In a recent interview with Bloomberg news, Eric Schmidt, former CEO of Google, explains Google's killing competitive advantage: having the right talent is everything in today's high-tech era.

- Identify the key decision maker and try to win her over.

- To incapacitate your competitor's organization, destroy the glue that holds it together.

- To impair your competitor, recruit its executives.

QUESTIONS TO CONSIDER

✓ *How are you recruiting top talent?*

✓ *Why would top talent want to come work for you?*

✓ *Where can you find the talent you need to advance your business?*

CHAPTER 4

Confusion Strategems

> ### *Stratagem 19:*
> ## Remove the Firewood from Under the Pot
>
> *When confronted with a strong opponent, do not fight him head-on, but try to find the spot that initiates a collapse, destroying his morale. This is how the weak can conquer the strong.*
>
> —The 36 Stratagems

LONG AGO IN CHINA

Confucius was made an important counselor to the lord of Lu state. This upset Lord Jing Gong of Qi state, a northern neighbor of Lu. For he feared that Confucius's reputable wisdom and influence would make Lu state a powerhouse and put Qi at risk of being annexed. He consulted his adviser on how to get rid of Confucius. Li Mi said, "Have you heard that one will think of sex when he is well fed and warm, and one will think of robbing others when he is desperate?" It was commonly known that the ruler of Lu was fond of women, so Li Mi gathered eighty beauties who were trained to dance and sing, to serve the lord of Lu. Jing Gong ordered them sent to the state of Lu as a present for the Lu ruler.

Both the ruler of Lu and his assistant were enchanted by the beauties. They showed up late to meetings and even rushed back to their women before the meetings were over. Confucius was very upset about this. After giving the ruler of Lu a few more chances, Confucius told his disciples to pack and leave the state of Lu.

Jing Gong got rid of Confucius, one of the most highly respected advisers anywhere, thus depriving the lord of Lu of a wise counselor and leaving his state vulnerable.

MODERN APPLICATIONS

Pulling the Anchor

In the business of developing and managing shopping centers, getting a solid anchor tenant is one of the key elements of success. Anchor tenants are the firewood that fuels the fire. But when the local market is saturated, it is nearly impossible to get a big-box anchor such as Walmart, Target, Kroger, or Home Depot into a newly built shopping center, since there is only so much population in a given area to support a retail giant. Persuading the anchor of an existing shopping center to move to a newly built location by offering preferential terms could be an effective stratagem. An anchor store such as a Walmart superstore or a grocery chain attracts traffic to the whole center and, in turn, the smaller shops. Thus, once the anchor moves, there is a good chance that small shops around it will follow.

Geek Squad Rescues Best Buy

Geek Squad caught my attention when a man in a uniform of black pants, white shirt, black tie, white socks, and black shoes walked out of a "Geekmobile"—a black-and-white-painted Volkswagen Beetle—and knocked at my neighbor's door.

Geek Squad was founded in 1994, on a budget of two hundred dollars, by Robert Stephens, who dropped out of his art and computer science program and rode around Minneapolis on his bicycle, helping people with computing problems. In 2002, with sixty agents and sales revenues of $3 million, he sold the company to Best Buy. Today, Geek Squad, with its 24,000 black-and-white-liveried tech experts and annual revenues of $1.5 billion, is the most well known brand of Best Buy, an electronics retailer that has been struggling because of the new e-commerce business model. Stephens once described Geek Squad as "a living comic book," inspired by *Star Wars,* video games, and cop shows. He borrowed the idea of wearing uniforms and using vehicles as marketing from UPS, and the idea of flat-rate pricing from Rapid Oil Change.

Geek Squad has been Best Buy's "killer differentiation," which sets it apart from other nationwide chains. And amid today's tight competition, it may be more critical than ever to the company's survival and growth. According to Trefis Team's article in the October 10, 2012, issue of *Forbes,* in addition to Best Buy's in-house technical service, it sells its Geek Squad services to other retailers. Ebay is offering customers a twenty-four-hour Geek Squad service plan package regardless of the electronics' buying origination. Target is rolling out Geek Squad service at twenty-eight of its stores. To compete against Walmart, Costco, and Amazon, which provide discounted electronics and attractive shipping offers, Best Buy continues to invest and capitalize on its strength in the services segment, which is the new "firewood" under its pot.

Sharp Taps into Sony's Forgotten Niche

The Japanese have long been known for taking pride in their "made in Japan" label. In the old days, Sony was the pride of Japan. Today, its products are outsourced in China, Thailand, and other developing countries, yet sold at premium prices. But this just won't do for the hard-core Japanese who are ready to pay a premium for the guaranteed high quality of "made in Japan" products.

Jake Adelstein and Nathalie-Kyoko Stucky wrote in an article on Japan Subculture Research Center's Web site that in 2004, Sharp opened its TV factories in Kageyama, Mie Prefecture. This came at a time when most Japanese electronics companies were starting to locate their factories overseas, to lower their assembly costs. In

2009, Sharp also opened similar factories in Yaita City in Tochigi Prefecture, and in Osaka. Televisions produced in Kageyama were called the "Kageyama model" TVs and enjoyed huge popularity among Japanese consumers. Sharp's "Kageyama model" TVs are twice the price of other TVs, but they sell well to people who really care about quality "made in Japan" products. Sharp cleverly filled the niche when Sony removed the "firewood"—the "made in Japan" label—from under its own "pot."

IMPLEMENTATION TACTICS

The literal translation of this stratagem advises taking away the firewood to stop the water in the pot from boiling. The essence is to eliminate the source of power. Sharp depleted Sony by stoking the Japanese demand for "made in Japan" products. In shopping center development, pulling out an anchor store—the "firewood"—from the competition to your center is sometimes the best way to attract other tenants. Geek Squad is the "firewood" under Best Buy's "pot."

A few key points to consider:

- When you are in an inferior position, avoid competing head-on.

- Identify and develop your own niche market, or "firewood."

- Identify and develop your competitive edge, which could make your enemy's strength and power irrelevant.

- Differentiate, and build on your existing strengths. Find what makes your competition strong, and prevent them from drawing on this resource. You can acquire it, destroy it, or disable it.

- Be creative! Find ways to sap the competition's strength by diminishing their morale.

QUESTIONS TO CONSIDER

✓ *What does your competition depend on? What is its source of power?*

✓ *How can you outflank your competition? How do you take away that source of power?*

✓ *What can you do to you make your competition's strength and power irrelevant?*

Stratagem 20:
Muddy the Water to Catch the Fish

In warfare, when the enemy is in chaos, exploit his weakened position and gain control when he has no direction.

—The 36 Stratagems

LONG AGO IN CHINA

When Cao Cao was fighting at Guan Du, his army ran out of supplies. He ordered his troops to steal supplies from the Yuan army. Cao Cao's frontline soldiers dressed like Yuan's army and carried the Yuan flag. When asked at the gate, they claimed that they were Yuan's reinforcements, coming from the home base. When they reached the warehouse, they set fire to some of the enemy's tents. The Yuan soldiers, too busy extinguishing the fire and unable to distinguish Cao Cao's army from their own, did not see Cao Cao's army advancing. In this way, Cao Cao gained control of the battle at Guan Du.

MODERN APPLICATIONS

The Art of Creating Confusion

On a trip to Beijing China, I told a taxi driver to take me to Walmart since I wanted to shop for a few items that I could not take with me on the airplane. In twenty minutes, he dropped me off right in front of a store—Wumart.

Many businesses not only borrow successful, well-branded business models but also "muddy the water" by choosing a brand name that is very close to that of a reputable company. For example,

Wumart Stores, a Chinese retailer with 430 convenience stores and hypermarkets, established in 1994, has the same business model as Walmart. Baidu's search engine replicates the same business model as Google's and uses very much the same clean search page as Google's. Best Buy Vietnam Co., a young Vietnamese retailer, has the same name and a similar logo design to that of Best Buy in the United States. By confusing the consumer—"muddying the water"—those brands attract consumers' attention and win faster exposure to the market. Today, in the e-commerce era, owning Internet domain names that are close to a well-established brand could be a lucrative business. The owner can use it to leverage an advantage, or sell it at a premium price.

Hyundai Wins America's Hearts and Minds

Hyundai entered the U.S. market in 1986. At that time, most automobile manufacturers had abandoned entry-level buyers to concentrate on high-end, high-priced vehicles, leaving a large void in the market. In February 1986, Hyundai launched its subcompact Excel model in the U.S. market. Success was instantaneous. Hyundai had filled in the void for first-time car buyers such as college students and young families, who could not find cars that met their needs yet were priced within their economic means. Total 1986 sales numbered 168,882—an industry record for an import car distributor in its first year. In 1987, Hyundai sales continued to soar, reaching a record 263,610 units. In 2007, Hyundai's U.S. market share was about 3 percent. Within two years, it soared to 5 percent as consumers discovered that Hyundai was building cars that matched or exceeded the quality of far more expensive luxury models.

Besides dedicating itself to making safe, reliable, high-quality cars at an affordable price, Hyundai is committed to building a car company that stands for more than a car company in the hearts and minds of its customers. Carmine Gallo wrote in *Forbes,* December 30, 2013, that one example was the buyback program rolled out in 2009. During the hardest time of the economic recession, Hyundai launched the "Assurance Program," a one-year guarantee to buy back a new Hyundai should the customer lose his or her job. It was a sensitive and risky move to run an advertising campaign, and build a brand, around job loss. Moreover, the buyback could drastically hurt sales revenue, especially during the depths of the recession. And yet, the risky campaign paid off. It was well received, and—even more important—customers felt deeply connected to the brand and its company's philosophy. The buyback program ended in 2011, but the "assurance" message struck a lasting positive emotional chord with the customers. Hyundai earned the "America's best warranty" designation. Hyundai had applied the stratagem in the best light, stepping into the "muddied water" of the recession and helping people out, thereby "catching the fish."

Rudy Giuliani, Hero of New York City

In 2008, I had a chance to hear Rudy Giuliani speak about leadership at a mega conference in Atlanta. He captivated the audience with vivid stories of how he had learned and developed leadership skills during his career as a U.S. attorney, two stints in the Justice Department, and two terms as mayor of the biggest city in the United States. He was perceived as a tough mayor and credited for improving the quality of life in the city by reducing crime. According to the City of New York's Web site, under Giuliani's leadership, overall crime was down 57 percent, murder was down 65 percent, and New York City—once infamous around the world for its dangerous streets—has been recognized by the FBI as the safest large city in America for five years straight.

And yet, Giuliani's leadership became prominent and gained international attention only in his last year as mayor, after the September 11, 2001, terrorist attacks. He was widely praised for his leadership during and after the crisis. When polled just six weeks after the attack, Giuliani received a 79 percent approval rating among New York City voters. This was a dramatic increase over the 36 percent rating he had gotten only the year before. Despite different points of view on Giuliani's leadership, the 9-11 crisis was a pivotal moment in his career. His influential leadership shone, and he won hearts and minds on a global scale. According to a Chinese saying, "Crisis gives birth to heroes." Giuliani is one of them.

Implementation Tactics

Crisis gives birth to heroes.

—Chinese proverb

This stratagem works in two distinctive situations: when there is already a state of chaos and confusion, and when there is not (yet) chaos. In the first situation, it is advisable to be opportunistic and "catch the fish" when the water is clouded with mud. The fish cannot see well and is slow to react; therefore, you can catch it more easily than when the water is clear. In the second situation, the stratagem suggests *creating* the confusion and then exploiting it to your advantage.

Leadership and Management.

- Taking on a leadership role is more effective and influential during times of uncertainty than when all is well.

- Influence your prospect in a chaotic time, for then he will be quicker to make an impulsive decision.

- Avoid confusion in your team and organization by providing a clear mission, vision, policy, communication, feedback, and motivation-and-reward system.

- Get your resources in reserve and your plans in place. If you plan ahead and stay alert, you will see opportunities when your competition begins to fall into disarray.

- Influence and create a lasting impression when your employees, customers, or counterparts are most vulnerable.

Sales and Marketing

- Vagueness can allow you room to maneuver.

- Bundle your products or services to create a perception in your favor.

- Confuse customers with details that distract them from their main concerns.

- Be alert to subtle changes that indicate confusion on the horizon, or signs of an opportunity to create confusion to your advantage.

QUESTIONS TO CONSIDER

✓ *How do you become the trusted adviser during difficult times?*

✓ *Do you have a clear vision, mission, and objectives that you live by?*

✓ *What can you do to take advantage of your competition's vulnerabilities?*

✓ *How effective is your team's communication, feedback, and rewards system?*

Stratagem 21:
Slough off the Cicada's Golden Shell

Preserve the original formation of the army and hold on to your position, so that your allies will not suspect your intention and the enemy will not will be roused to attack. Then withdraw and divert your force to attack from a different direction.

—The 36 Stratagems

LONG AGO IN CHINA

In the early second century B.C., during the West Han era, Xiang Yu of the Chu led his troops to attack Liu Bang. He cornered Liu Bang in the fortified city of Xing Yang. As the days went by and the food and supplies diminished, the situation looked desperate for Liu Bang and the Han soldiers. Then one of Liu Bang's generals proposed a ruse to allow Liu Bang to escape. The general had two thousand women dress as armored soldiers. Just before dawn, they took up battle formation, with the general sitting in the lord's carriage. Disguised as Emperor Liu Bang, the general signaled surrender, claiming that they had run of food. The Chu soldiers were overjoyed at the news. Meanwhile, Liu Bang quietly escaped with ten soldiers through the west gate. When Xiang Yu realized that he had been tricked, he had the general burned to death. But Liu Bang, the Han emperor, was saved.

MODERN APPLICATIONS

Companies such as Batteries Plus and Goodyear have been very successful operating on a model of franchising the companies' stores. As long as they operate consistently and standardize products and services, customers cannot tell the difference between one franchise and another.

Marriott Sloughs Off Its Golden Shell

In the late 1980s, after Marriott had become one of the largest commercial real estate developers and borrowers in the United States, the company went through a gloomy period, when it accounted for one-third of the collapse in new-hotel commercial real estate. In the process of resolving the real estate disaster, Bill Marriott, then CEO of Marriott Corporation, hired Stephen Bollenbach, who worked out a deal on Donald Trump's property and got banks to write off Trump's debt. Bollenbach applied the "Slough off the cicada's golden shell" stratagem effectively by splitting Marriott Corporation into two arms: situating its real estate and debt in Host Marriott and creating a hotel-management company, Marriott International. The strategy alleviated the Marriott Corporation's debt burden, allowed Marriott International to focus on its core competence—providing customer service—and sped up its global expansion without financial risk. Marriott became the world's largest hotel-management company. It has expanded into 74 countries, managing 660,000 hotel rooms under 19 different brands, from the luxury Ritz-Carlton to Marriott Hotels in the middle range, to Holiday Inns at the lower end. During the next three years, it plans to develop a new hotel every month in China.

According to a July 2013 *Forbes* article by Halah Touryalai, in 2012 Marriott owned only 10 of the 3,800 properties under its control. Even though it does not own hotels, Marriott International netted $571 million in profits generated from providing customer service and management. Marriott applies a 3-and-25 fee structure (3-and-10 in Asia). That is, it charges the hotel owners around 3 percent of a hotel's sales, plus 25 percent of profits (10 percent of profits in Asia). Hotel owners pay Marriott for almost everything, including renovation costs, revenue management and accounting, sales, and marketing.

In the operation of hotel properties, international management brands use this stratagem to the fullest. Without taking any equity stake (or the attendant risks), a branded hotel management company charges fees on revenue, profits, food, and so on.

Will Maserati's New Golden Shell Entice German-Car Lovers?

Maserati has long supplied exotic and exorbitantly priced cars to the "filthy rich." According to Tommaso Ebhardt in Bloomberg Businessweek (July 3, 2013), now the luxury sports-car brand is shifting its focus to the *merely rich*. Why not? Maserati has that Italian sex appeal backed by the power and cachet of engines from the Ferrari family brand. The Ghibli (Arabic word meaning hot wind from the Sahara) features a 330-horsepower V-6 engine by Ferrari, and its luxury interior is accented with Italian leather Poltrona Frau. Trying to go after the most expensive German-made cars—including Audi A6, BMW, and Mercedes E550—Ghibli, starting at $65,600, will cost about 20 percent more than the same-size German sedan. Experts in the industry predict that beating the Germans won't be easy and that Maserati's price range is on the high side for a midsize luxury sedan. But Maserati believes that with its elite heritage, its differentiation from the German models, and the right quality and distribution network, it can reach its goal of selling 20,000 Ghibli sedans in 2015.

Meanwhile, Fiat, which owns Maserati, Chrysler, Lancia, Alfa Romeo, and Ferrari, is losing money in Europe (to the tune of more than 700 million euros in 2012). Fiat is counting on sales of the higher- margin luxury cars overseas to keep its plants running. Fiat is investing $1.6 billion to revamp Maserati—the "cicada." If it succeeds, Ghibli could be the "golden shell" that creates a perfect facade for Fiat.

IMPLEMENTATION TACTICS

Hence, when able to attack, we must seem unable; when using our forces, we must seem inactive; when we are near, we must make the enemy believe we are far away; when far away, we must make him believe we are near.

—Sun Tzu

When a cicada metamorphoses, it sheds its skin, which glints like gold in the sunlight, and escapes unnoticed. When you keep things unchanged on the surface, the enemy may not notice the internal changes, and this enables the execution of your main plans, whether they involve retreat, expansion, or counterattack. This stratagem has been applied internationally in many other services, including training, management consulting, legal and accounting.

Major clothing and fashion companies such as Ralph Lauren use the same trick. Ralph Lauren is a fashion pioneer who ingratiated himself with consumers through lifestyle branding. He did this by leveraging his "cicada skin": brand recognition. Then the company "shed its skin"—selling its license to other clothing manufacturers to produce merchandise at different price points, with brands including Polo, Rugby, Club Monaco, Lauren, and Chaps.

Leadership and Management

- Develop your people to replace you, and phase yourself out of running day-to-day activities to focus on more strategic or value-added tasks.

- Develop a contingency plan to back up your main plan. If the main plan doesn't work out as planned, a well-thought-out contingency plan helps reduce disruption in your organization since it appears as the main plan.

Business

Marriott uses Marriott International as a golden shell to cover the Marriott Corporation's debt burden. Maserati sloughs off its golden skin, creating a Ghibli to cover for Fiat's losing business in Europe. In wartime, Sun Tzu advised on how to battle on different kinds of terrain: soft and hard. In business, gain and loss are inevitable when a business operates across dimensions (products, markets, industries). So, by creating a facade—a "golden shell"—you can cover a loss or hide the real action and manipulate your competition.

- Have a mixture of company-owned store operations and franchisees to strengthen the brand while lowering costs and reducing risk.

- Develop a facade, or "golden shell," to cover the loss or manipulate your competition.

- Partner with those who have the strengths that you lack.

- When reducing your stake or investment in an organization, take on an advisory role so your withdrawal will not cause alarm.

- In negotiation, use the "good cop, bad cop" stratagem to confuse your counterpart. One acts as a decoy, the other as a striking force.

QUESTIONS TO CONSIDER

✓ *What is your contingency plan?*

✓ *If you have no contingency plan (or an incomplete one), how do you plan to create one?*

✓ *What are your business's soft and hard spots?*

✓ *What facade can you build to cover the soft spots?*

✓ *What facade can you create to avoid stirring up the competition?*

✓ *How do you create that "glint of gold"?*

Stratagem 22:
Shut the Doors to Trap the Thief

When dealing with a weak but agile enemy,
surround him to trap him. Don't exhaust yourself
by pursuing him, since you may be ambushed.

—The 36 Stratagems

LONG AGO IN CHINA

In 260 B.C., the two states Qin and Zhao were at war. The armies of the two states were locked in a stalemate when Qin applied the "Shut the doors to trap the thief" stratagem. The Qin attacked the Zhao army, then feigned a retreat so that the Zhao army pursued them. The new commander of the Zhao pushed the troops into Qin territory, only to find out that the Qin army had retreated to the sides and had gathered behind the Zhao forces. They were trapped for a month and could find no way out. As supplies ran out, the troops grew weak and desperate. The commander of Zhao gathered his best men to make a final attempt to break free. He was killed, leaving his starving soldiers desperate and directionless. The Qin easily attacked the poor Zhao soldiers and killed them all.

MODERN APPLICATIONS

The Trap of Amazon's One-Click Technology

As I juggle a busy life, the last thing I need when trying to buy something on the Web is to have to fumble through my wallet to get a credit card, then key the info only to make an error, get rejected, do it over again, then go through multiple pages to get to the checkout and buy the product. Amazon provides a seamless one-click checkout—an enjoyable, no-fuss customer experience. I admit it. I am trapped since Amazon offers the solution for my pain: the one-click checkout. Since Amazon stores the customer's payment and shipping information on its server, it has the capability to validate customers' credentials and convert them to "one-click checkout" customers. The feature lets returning customers buy items simply by clicking a mouse button, without having to reenter a shipping address or credit card number. This easy, frictionless one-click buying experience is an adaptation of the "Shut the doors to trap the thief" stratagem. A customer goes to Amazon to buy merchandise because of the competitive pricing, fast delivery, and, above all, convenience. Once she uses the frictionless one-click checkout, there is an excellent chance that she will repeat the experience. Even Apple adopted the strategy. In 2000, it licensed Amazon's one-click patent and incorporated it into iTunes, iPhoto, and the Apple App Store. Besides enhancing the customer's experience, the one-click technology induces an impulsive buying decision without much of a second thought—after all, it's so *easy.* Instant purchases and one-click convenience drive sales and retain customer loyalty. Amazon and Apple use the one-click technology as the "shutting door" to "trap" the customer. My 4-year-old, Levi, uses this stratagem on me. Every time he wants to buy a new app on iTunes, he says, "Mommy, it's only one click."

Samsung's Value Chain "Trap"

Part of Samsung's killer "secret sauce" is its value chain—the integration system for key components such as semiconductors and LCD panels used in its end products. For instance, the dynamic random access memory, flash memory, and mobile phone chips manufactured by Samsung's semiconductor business supply the company's computer, communication, digital home appliance, and living home appliance divisions. The component divisions collaborate closely with end-product businesses, thus eliminating a lot of waste. On top of supplying to Samsung's internal businesses, divisions that specialize in components such as Samsung Corning and Samsung Electro-Mechanics also supply to the competition to maximize profits. (Apple is one of its largest component customers.) This integrated system lowers procurement costs and improves speed of design, development, and production. While all its competitors must rely on third parties to accomplish the same tasks, Samsung controls and manufactures many of the building blocks of its end products such as TV and phones. The integrated control of all operations creates an impenetrable "trap" for Samsung to churn out new products fast, efficiently, and seamlessly. Indeed, the integrated "trap" (value chain) is one of Samsung Electronics' core competencies.

FaceBook to Pay $16 Billion to Fortify the "Trap"

Remember MySpace? I do . . . vaguely. MySpace, the pioneer in social networking, has fallen into oblivion. As Facebook, the mighty social network, turned ten years old in May 2013, many experts in the industry started to question its "awkward puberty," asking if it would vanish as MySpace did. Today, Internet users, especially young people, crave new and different sorts of online experience while connecting with one another. Facebook's rivals such as Snapchat and Twitter, with different approaches to private and public sharing, have grown at a rate that Facebook surely finds alarming. In fact, my colleagues strategically advised me to switch to Twitter, and my 25-year-old nephew insisted that I need to try the new and cool Snapchat. With major rivals as well as Internet startups offering users more and more social platforms, Facebook is having difficulty attracting new users and keeping the existing ones *engaged.*

Amid today's abundance of information, keeping people engaged is a daunting task. If Facebook does not find a way not only to attract new users but also to "shut the doors and trap them," it will continue losing ground to other trendy social networking rivals. Brad Stone and Sarah Frier wrote in *Bloomberg Businessweek* (February 2014) that acquiring Instagram in spring 2012 for $1 billion to keep Facebook interesting was not enough, so Facebook is steering into the domain of Google. It attempts to harvest all the data to provide answers to most questions online. For instance, if you ask your friends for the name of a good local bakery or doctor, Facebook strives to generate answers just as Google does. To really "shut the doors," Mark Zuckerberg's strategic plan for 2014 is all about strengthening Facebook's presence in mobile—"the trap"—where people communicate, do business, and connect, and which they basically cannot do without. Seeking new ways to be an instant player in mobile messaging, Facebook announced on February 20, 2014 that it would acquire the fast-growing WhatsApp firm for $16 billion in cash and stock. WhatsApp is a cross-platform mobile messaging app that works on all major smartphone operating systems, providing its users with a new short message service (SMS) alternative. Facebook released the rationale behind this huge acquisition it wants to make:

- Over 450 million people use WhatsApp each month.

- Seventy percent of those people are active on any given day.

- Messaging volume approaches the entire global telecom SMS volume.

- It enjoys continued strong growth, currently adding more than a million new registered users per day.

Keeping customers and users engaged by luring them in with attractive bait—"shutting the doors and trapping them"—is a critical stratagem for a social platform to survive and thrive.

IMPLEMENTATION TACTICS

This stratagem advises containing an adversary rather than attacking him directly, tempting him into situations where his own actions will only cause him further trouble. When you surround him, you prevent him from either launching another attack against you or running away. The essence is exploiting the *isolated position* that they have voluntarily entered or have been enticed to. This tactic is considered effective when you are in the stronger position. That way, you can prevent your enemy from doing you any more harm, while preserving your energy and resources. In business, create an enclosure that is impenetrable, fortified, and inescapable. Samsung's integrated system (value chain) is a compelling illustration of the stratagem. It enables Samsung to operate as a seamless manufacturer that barely relies on third parties, while serving as a "trap" to its competitors, who must rely on it. Also, *contain* your customers by constantly engaging them, making them never lose interest in your product or service. The above examples suggest that Facebook and Amazon are determined to be around for a long time. Remember:

- Offer significant added value to keep your customers engaged.

- Captivate your customers by catering to their needs and solving their problems.

- Engage customers by continually being interesting and reinventing yourself and your brand.

QUESTIONS TO CONSIDER

✓ *What action do you need to take to retain customers?*

✓ *What threat of luring your customers away does your competition pose?*

✓ *How and when can you most efficiently and effectively influence your customers and your competition?*

✓ *How can you make it easier for your customers to do business with you?*

✓ *What innovation could you develop to hold on to your customers?*

Stratagem 23:
Befriend the Far and Attack the Near

*Because of geographical constraints, it is
more advantageous to attack a nearby enemy
than another far away. Ally yourself with your
distant enemy temporarily, despite your differences.*

—The 36 Stratagems

LONG AGO IN CHINA

During the Warring States period, every state pursued dominance over others in the hope of expanding its wealth and influence. Qin was the largest and most powerful state of all. In fear of Qin's might, smaller neighboring states allied to protect themselves from being attacked. Despite being a powerful state, Qin would not have an easy time attacking the united smaller neighboring states, because powerful distant states would come to their defense if Qin attempted to assault them. To conquer distant states was equally hard for Qin since the food, logistics, and fatigue involved in a long journey would put a traveling army at a serious disadvantage. To break the deadlock, Qin state's adviser proposed an unorthodox stratagem.

Qin sent messages to faraway states Chu and Qi, saying that it had no reason to attack them and, in fact, was interested in forming an alliance with them to attack Qin's neighboring states. This made them feel secure, and so they neglected forming strong alliances for defense. Having the support of the distant states, Qin was able to focus its resources and strength on attacking the small neighboring states one by one. First, it attacked Han, then Wei and Zhao, incorporating their small territory while amassing greater power. Then Qin used these conquests as reinforcements to attack more distant states, such as Yan, and Chu and, finally, Qi. The contentious battles of 250 years among the seven kingdoms ceased, and for the first time in history, China was unified under a single ruler: Qin.

MODERN APPLICATIONS

Befriend the Far to Avoid Taxes

Companies commonly use this stratagem to avoid taxes. The company sets up a "mailbox" company or subsidiary in a low-tax country such as Ireland, Luxembourg, Netherlands, Cayman Islands, or British Virgin Islands. In the United States, Nevada is famous having no state income tax and no capital gains tax. Apple's headquarters are in Cupertino, California. But by putting an office in Reno, Nevada, Apple can avoid California's 8.84 percent corporate tax rate and pay zero tax in Nevada. Many other companies, such as Cisco, Harley-Davidson, and Microsoft, have also set up subsidiaries in Nevada to bypass taxes in other states.

In *New York Times* article (April 28, 2012), Charles Duhigg and David Kocieniewski write that Apple was the pioneer in the accounting tactic known as the "double Irish with a Dutch sandwich" accounting scheme, which routes profits through subsidiaries in low-tax Ireland and the Netherlands and then to a tax-free Caribbean nation. Apple has managed legal ways to allocate about 70 percent of its profits overseas, where tax rates are much lower. Today, the tactic is being copied by hundreds of corporations worldwide.

Luxembourg, for instant, offers favorable taxes to lure businesses to this small country of half a million people. In 2011, iTunes Luxembourg's revenue exceeded $1 billion, making up for 20 percent of iTunes' worldwide sales. In this digital age, unlike with sales of physical goods, when a song, app, or software is downloaded anywhere in the world, the transaction can be routed to Luxembourg to benefit from the discounted tax rate there, avoiding the much higher tax in the country where the transaction actually takes place.

In Ireland, to benefit from business and job creation, the government offered tax breaks to tech companies such as Apple.

The biggest advantage for the company is the tax haven that it can move profits to. By moving funds from one country to another, a company reaps tax savings. For example, some profits were taxed at the Irish rate of 12.5 percent versus the American rate of 35 percent. Thus, it's no surprise that this small country of five million people accounts for one-third of Apple's global revenues.

Also, companies in high-tax countries such as Germany and the UK have used Singapore as a designated distributor. For example, a sales representative in the high-tax UK could sell a product or service on behalf of a designated subsidiary in low-tax Singapore. Taiwanese companies and even mainland Chinese companies have used Hong Kong heavily as a base to conduct business with China. By "befriending the far"—basing in Hong Kong, which offers liberal commerce regulations and a favorable tax rate—these companies can "attack the near" by gaining an advantage over the competition via tax savings and freedom from the Chinese mainland's many areas of restriction.

Besides tax avoidance, "befriend the far and attack the near" can be used to go around a system. Ebay China folded in 2006 for many reasons, among them the inability to replicate Ebay's success in North America. Chinese banking and financial restrictions did not allow Ebay to be nimble. To learn the lesson, Ebay joined hands with Tom Media, run by Hong Kong billionaire Li Ka Shing. After years of tug-of-war with the government in China, Google decided to shut down the Google.cn site and redirect traffic to its service at Google.hk in Hong Kong. Thanks to Hong Kong's history as a free-trade zone, Google did not have to comply with the restrictions and censorship of the government in mainland China. The Chinese government was not satisfied with Google's approach. Therefore, Google changed its landing page so that users could no longer be taken directly to Google.hk but had to click on a link to it. From this link, Google would provide uncensored search.

Befriend the Far to Survive and Expand

In the early 1970s, Singapore was abandoned by the UK and estranged from Malaysia, had opposite political views from

Vietnam and China, and had a tense relationship with Indonesia. So Singapore allied with a distant powerhouse, the United States. It proved to be a smart move by Singapore's leadership. The influx of U.S.-based multinational corporations' direct investment in the country played a central role in restoring and rebuilding Singapore.

Israel prevailed over its Muslim neighbors, in part by heavily exploiting this stratagem, by allying itself with the United States in North America, and the UK in Europe.

Many U. S. companies and chains, unable to compete in the North American market, either vanish at home or have an underdog position there, yet still have a strong position and make profits in foreign markets. These companies include Burger King, Häagen Dazs, and Baskin Robbins, to name but a few.

When their popularity wanes due to new competition in a cutthroat industry, singers such as Gwen Stefani and Pink ally with musical organizations in Japan and South Korea to capture different segments of the market, then come back to the United States as more accomplished global artists with a new fan base.

IMPLEMENTATION TACTICS

This stratagem is widely used in today's complex globalized environment. Samsung and Sony are rivals in certain areas, competing to sell their end products, but join forces to produce parts or supply each other, thereby enjoying economies of scale and cost efficiency to thwart competition on price. FedEx and UPS use the United States Postal Service (USPS) to deliver packages to remote areas where they don't want to expand operations and where USPS already has established routes. It is more efficient for these carriers to outsource to their competitor, USPS. Using strategic alliances to "befriend the far and attack the near" is also popular in the airline industry, auto manufacturing, and shipping. By joining forces and sharing hubs, facilities, and networks, businesses in these industries can grow globally while lowering costs. Each can be more efficient and competitive in its own local and regional markets.

Bear these points in mind:

- Identify the right enemy and partner with him to achieve a specific goal.

- Seek to disrupt alliances that threaten you, while creating alliances that offer you power (yet always beware lest your allies change sides due to external or internal circumstances).

- Joint ventures, partnerships, licensing, or franchising can be a cost-effective entrée to distant places, enabling you to avoid overcrowded marketplaces with fierce competition.

- Leverage technology such as Internet, social media, e-commerce, and cloud computing to gain a global presence.

- Avoid overcrowded markets and intense competition by operating in underserved segments.

- Steadily expand your empire/market, and eventually you will gather enough scale and scope to conquer the tougher "distant" competition.

QUESTIONS TO CONSIDER

✓ *Who is your competition? Identify as many as you can.*

✓ *Find out common goals that will help both of you beat the other competition.*

✓ *How can you ally and cooperate with your identified competitor to achieve a common goal?*

✓ *Which battle would you jointly fight? Which common goal(s) would you jointly achieve, and how?*

Stratagem 24:
Borrow a Road to Conquer Guo

When a smaller state, located between the enemy and yourself, is being threatened by the enemy state, immediately send support to the smaller state, thereby exerting your influence over him. Mere talk without action will not win the trust of a small state in a precarious position.

—The 36 Stratagems

LONG AGO IN CHINA

During the Spring and Autumn period, two small neighboring states, Yu and Guo, bordered the larger, more powerful kingdom of Jin. Jin had ambitions to conquer the neighboring states and expand its territory. The lord of Jin bribed Yu's leader, who was known to be corrupt, with a lavish party and gifts in exchange for passage through Yu to attack Guo. His adviser warned him that the gifts were not without strings and that if Guo was conquered, Yu would be in a disadvantageous position. Yu's leader ignored the warning. He accepted the gifts and let the Jin army pass through his territory to attack Guo.

The Jin army captured Guo in a surprise attack and, on its way home, attacked and conquered Yu.

MODERN APPLICATIONS

Asian Tigers Borrow Many Roads to Conquer the World

After the Second World War, Japan's economy was in ruins. It was not taken seriously or perceived as an economic threat to the United States. Indeed, the United States actually contributed to restoring Japan's economy under the Marshall Plan. To establish a foothold, Japan sold its products under Western brand names. By "borrowing a road," Japan has learned the best practices in management, leadership, marketing, distribution channels, and technology from the best global firms and has gained access to world markets. In fifty years, the Japanese have built global brands including Toyota, Honda, Sony, Mitsubishi, Itochu, and a slew of others.

Meanwhile, Korea has emulated the Japanese model. This has led Koreans to establish global brands including Samsung, LG Electronics, Hyundai, and Kia in less than thirty years.

Then came the Chinese. By applying the same model, Lenovo, a Chinese multinational electronics corporation founded in Beijing in 1984, has shortened the learning curve even more. The company has borrowed many roads, which led it from its ill-timed and inauspicious beginnings to becoming the world's third-largest computer manufacturer—in only fifteen years!

Lenovo became the largest distributor of Hewlett-Packard computers and Toshiba notebooks in China. This enabled it to absorb the best practices of the international manufacturers, including leadership and management practices, strategies for attracting and retaining talent, customer service excellence, strategic distribution logistics, and vendor channel management. Along the way, Lenovo evolved and developed a deep understanding of Chinese consumer behaviors. Borrowing commercial and technological knowledge from its alliances with HP and many other international firms, it continued to grow, and by the early 2000s, it had captured 30 percent of the market share in China.

To increase its global dominance, Lenovo continued to "borrow many roads" to conquer the world. The company is known for a number of high-profile acquisitions. In 2005, it paid $1.25 billion in cash and stock to acquire IBM's PC business, accelerating Lenovo's access to foreign markets. Liu Chuanzhi said, "We benefited in three ways from the IBM acquisition. We got the ThinkPad brand, IBM's more advanced PC manufacturing technology, and the company's international resources, such as its global sales channels and operation teams. These three elements have shored up our sales revenue in the past several years."

In 2011, Lenovo formed a PC joint venture with Japanese information technology giant NEC. This joint venture is intended to boost Lenovo's worldwide sales by expanding its presence in Japan, a key market for personal computers. In the same year, Lenovo acquired Medion, a German electronics manufacturing company. Lenovo said the acquisition would double its share of the German computer market, making it the third-largest vendor by sales (after Acer and HP). In September 2012, Lenovo agreed to acquire the U.S.-based software company Stoneware. More specifically, Stoneware was acquired to further Lenovo's efforts to improve and expand its cloud-computing services. In January 2014, Lenovo agreed to acquire IBM's low-end server business for $2.3 billion. This deal put Lenovo in the world's third-largest server brand position.

Bruce Einhorn writes in *Bloomberg Businessweek* (January 30, 2014) that while other PC brands such as Hewlett-Packard, Dell, and Acer have had little success with mobile devices, Lenovo becomes the world's fourth-largest smartphone brand. By "borrowing a road" from Google—acquiring Google's technology (Motorola Mobility) for $3 billion—Lenovo is on the move to take further strides in "conquering" the mobile industry.

On Jan. 28th 2014, to take on rivals Apple and Samsung, Lenovo announced that it was structuring itself into four main business groups—PCs, mobile devices, servers and storage, and cloud service. Lenovo CEO Yang said that the new structure "will help us be even faster, more focused, and more efficient."

The Transrapid in Shanghai

In March 2013, I had the opportunity to check out the fastest train in the world, the Transrapid, which travels from Pudong Airport to downtown Shanghai. While the literature gave me an impression of China's pride in its magnetic suspension technology, the reality is that Transrapid was built on a "borrowed road." In June 2000, the Chinese prime minister visited Germany and traveled on a test magnetic suspension track in Lathen, Emsland. He was impressed with the technology and decided to have the 18.6-mile Transrapid built in Shanghai. In January 2001, the city of Shanghai and Transrapid International signed a contract committing them to use German magnetic suspension technology and the mostly German-made components for the Transrapid. But during a test run, there was minor damage due to overheated magnetic motors. According to Harro Vo Senger in his book *The 36 Stratagems for Business*, The Chinese took this opportunity to pressure Siemens and ThyssenKrupp, the German contractors, to transfer German technology to China so that the Chinese partner could develop and adapt it. The Chinese blamed German technology for failing to solve the issues caused by temperature fluctuation, movement of concrete, and the muddy ground in Shanghai. Faced with the fait-accompli contract and commitment, the German contractors reluctantly had to transfer essential patents. The Germans became component suppliers of their own high-speed technology, while most of it was produced in China. As a result, China is now proudly showing the world its improved magnetic suspension technology.

IMPLEMENTATION TACTICS

This stratagem suggests entering alliances for mutual gain but not forgetting to build your own strength just in case the join venture should fall apart. Any relationship has uncontrollable elements. Using your ally as a "borrowed road," you can further your own goals without relying on the longevity of the relationship. Hyundai pulled off the Ford-apprentice relationship, becoming a dominant force and Ford's direct competitor. Lenovo and Samsung have used the same tactic.

Brand Leveraging

- Network in high-level associations.
- Name-drop.
- Use testimonials from well-known clients or organizations.
- Join influential groups and prestigious associations, and use this influence to enhance your positioning.
- Cobrand and coauthor for mutual benefit.

Business Expansion

- Take an apprenticeship to learn the tricks of the trade.
- Accept a minor, inferior role to get a foot in the door.

QUESTIONS TO CONSIDER

✓ *Identify companies, people, organizations, and experts that can help you reach your goal.*

✓ *What "borrowed road" is the best fit for your situation?*

✓ *How could you ally or partner with them to achieve your goal?*

Deception Strategems

LONG AGO IN CHINA

Emperor Qin fell gravely ill. Knowing that he would not live much longer, he wrote a will to his eldest son, Prince Fu, asking Fu to succeed him after his death. He left the letter with his most-trusted official, Zhao Cao, trusting that Zhao Cao would handle the transition smoothly and groom Prince Fu for the throne. He also anticipated that the news of his coming death would lead to civil war among the lords, and chaos in the land. So he stayed in a carriage, having servants continue to deliver food to the carriage while his officials conduct daily meetings next to the carriage, with the dying emperor and even after his death. Only Zhao Cao knew the whole truth, but he never gave the letter to Prince Fu.

Concerned about the succession to the throne, Li Si, the

prime minister, asked Zhao Cao for advice. Zhao Cao was also the favorite mentor of Prince Hu, the emperor's youngest son. He knew that if Prince Hu should accede to the throne, he himself would benefit from tremendous favor and power. Zhao Cao therefore advised Li Si, and together they nudged Prince Hu to get involved in a grand scheme. They changed the will so that it condemned Prince Fu to drink poison. Prince Hu then took the throne and named his favorite mentor, Zhao Cao, as his prime minister. Zhao Cao then killed Li Si to cover the truth.

MODERN APPLICATIONS

Baidu, the Google of China

While sitting in my room at the Beijing Hilton in March 2013, to my surprise, I could not get access to my Youtube videos or update my friends and family about my China journey on Facebook. And when I tried to do a Google search, I was somehow mysteriously diverted to a local Baidu search engine. Coming from America, I felt stifled without access to those familiar media. But my Chinese colleagues and students proudly told me, "Not a big deal! We have Baidu, China's Google; Renren, China's Facebook; and Sina Weibo, China's Twitter. Life is good here!" Some other tech-savvy friends showed me how to get around China's firewall through some private network portals, but it was just too cumbersome for a low-tech person like me to maneuver. Moreover, even if I could break through the firewall, it would still be a pain in the neck because the site dropped out every five or six minutes.

Baidu (Google), Renren (Facebook), Dengdeng (Amazon), Sina Weibu (Twitter), Alibaba (Ebay), and Xiaomi (Apple) are successful illustrations of how to "steal the beam" (the American business model and technology) and replace it with something else in today's global competition. Let's see how Baidu thwarts GoogleChina.

In 1994, Robin Li, a bright undergrad at Beijing University, was granted a fellowship at the State University of New York, Buffalo, for a master's degree in computer science, concentrating on information retrieval—the root of search. Li worked for IDD Enterprises, an online financial data service, as a senior consultant. When working on a project that involved developing software for the online edition of the *Wall Street Journal,* Li figured out a computerized method for sorting through vast amounts of data on the internet by ranking Web sites according to the related links. His search technology got no interest at Dow Jones, but he got a patent in the United States. In 1997, he left IDD and worked with Infoseek. In 1999, he left for China when Disney acquired Infoseek, and his project was sidelined. Li and his partner founded Baidu (Seeking Truth) and opened their office in Beijing in January 2000. According to Rebecca A. Fannin in her book *Silicon Dragons,* Li raised funds from venture capitalists in Silicon Valley, borrowing the idea that made Silicon Valley a hot spot: stock options for new staffers. Before figuring out the winning strategy, Li imitated three big U.S. tech companies at the time, including Inktomi, Akamai Technologies, and Verity. When Li looked at Google, which had started to monetize its business through search, he knew that Baidu needed to change its business model.

Li started by imitating the clean-looking, sparse Google interface. Rumor has it that Baidu's logo, a dog's footprint, was inspired by the Google sound. "Gou" means "dog" in Chinese. By educating newly capitalistic businesses about the power of online marketing and setting up a national network of advertising resellers in some two hundred major cities, Baidu began to make a profit in 2004.

In 2005, Google set up an office in China. There are two versions for Google search in China's market: Goole.cn, a Mandarin-language search engine run from China, and Google. com, run from California. But Baidu continued to outsmart Google in China for many reasons, one of which is that Baidu's algorithm is more relevant in Mandarin than Google's is. Google has hired a hundred engineers in China to improve its Mandarin-language search capabilities. The challenge it faces is to find simpler ways for users to input Pinyin (roman script) that signifies precisely in Mandarin.

Moreover, the Chinese government's strict censorship regulations are the major barrier against Google's entering China in a big way. According to CNZZ Web analytics, in August 2013, Baidu has a 63.16 percent market share in China, Google had 2.88 percent, and others had 33.96 percent. On the other hand, according to *Fortune* magazine, globally, Google has 65.6 percent, Baidu has 8.6 percent, and others have 25.8 percent.

Baidu has "stolen the beam" but replaced it with an even better timber. It had borrowed Silicon Valley's business model and adapted Google's technology to suit the Chinese mind and the Mandarin language.

Counterfeit Products from China to Bordering Countries

In August 2013, on a trip to Vietnam, I was invited to a friend's home for dinner. After awaiting a delicious dinner together, we looked in dismay at the mushy cooked rice—like melted rubber in the rice cooker. Duyen, living an hour away from Ho Chi Minh City center, is the housewife of a low-income family. The morning before, she went as usual to the "wet market" to shop for the day. She was invited to buy a new kind of rice that looked nice and cost one-third the usual price. Happy with the deal, she bought ten pounds to try it out.

The heavy metal cadmium in rice, plastic rice, toxins in milk, arsenic in soy sauce, exploding watermelons, fake eggs, rubber shrimp, bleach in mushrooms, a chemical to give meat a better appearance or turn pork to beef or turn rat to mutton—these are but a few horror stories involving imported or smuggled products from China. This raises concerns not only about China's poor food safety regulations but also about ethical and moral standards.

Vietnam experiences firsthand the consequences of fake

products smuggled over the Vietnam-China border. Made-in-China fake eggs, for instance, at one-tenth the price of eggs farmed in Vietnam, literally killed the Vietnamese egg-farming industry.

The worst case in China, in 2008, involved milk baby formula made with melamine, a poisonous plastic compound. Six infants died from drinking the milk, while more than 300,000 suffered kidney problems.

Honey: The Biggest Food Fraud in U.S. History

According to Susan Berfield in *Bloomberg Businessweek* (September 19, 2013), in 2001, after U.S. beekeepers accused Chinese companies of selling their honey at unfairly low prices, the U.S. government imposed import duties of as much as three times the price on Chinese honey. Since then, almost no honey comes from China legally.

ALW, a German-based company, used a network of brokers in China and Taiwan, who shipped honey from China to India, Indonesia, Malaysia, Thailand, Taiwan, the Philippines, South Korea, and Mongolia. Some of the honey was adulterated with sugar, syrup, and molasses to dull the tart flavor. Chinese honey is often harvested early and dried by machine rather than by bees, which allows the bees to produce more honey, but the honey has a smell and tastes a bit sour. In some cases, the honey was contaminated with residue of antibiotics such as chloramphenicol, which is banned in the United States. In March 2008, the Department of Homeland Security raided ALW's office in Chicago after U.S. honey producers warned Homeland Security that companies might be smuggling in honey from China. The unusually low prices and the sudden large influx of honey from Indonesia, Malaysia, and India—more than those countries historically produced—raised suspicions. In June, federal agents seized thousands more files from ALW's offices in Chicago and charged the two German representatives with conspiring to import mislabeled and adulterated honey from China. The Department of Justice accused the company and its affiliates and several brokers of evading $180 million in tariffs.

IMPLEMENTATION TACTICS

This stratagem, originally, is a deceptive one that suggests replacing something real with a fake. This was used in wartime, when winning is a zero-sum game. And, unfortunately, it is still commonly used in many parts of the world. In a business environment, where we have constitutions, laws, and ethics, this stratagem advises creating, innovating, or tweaking to make a better product, or it could involve disrupting a current trend or technology. Baidu is a good illustration: it replaced Google in the China market. Viber has disrupted Skype. Walmart continually copycats branded products and has its private label make the same product at a much cheaper price. This has long been one of Walmart's competitive advantages.

Critical Thinking

- Don't assume that people have the same ethical and moral standard as yours.

- Be skeptical of anything that seems too good or too cheap to be true.

- Use your critical thinking to avoid falling into the deception trap.

Business Development and "Disruptive Innovation"

The concept "disruptive innovation" was originally described by Dr. Clayton Christensen, a Harvard professor, in his 1997 book *Innovator's Dilemma*. It maintains that disruptive innovation begins with lower-quality and less desirable versions of products and services or in simple application in the bottom of the market. As the "disruptive innovators" relentlessly improve, they will move up the market and gain the attention of the main customer population, and eventually supplanting established competitors.

QUESTIONS TO CONSIDER

✓ *What are your competitor's core competencies?*

✓ *How can you approach and attack these core competencies?*

✓ *What "replacement timbers" do you have? How do you make those "timbers" work as well as the "beams"?*

Stratagem 26:
Point at the Mulberry Tree
While Scolding the Locust Tree

*A stronger force can sound a warning to
rule over the weak. One's uncompromising
display of power will earn support, and
resolute action will demand reverence.*

—The 36 Stratagems

LONG AGO IN CHINA

Emperor He Lu was pleased with Sun Tzu's war strategies and asked him for a demonstration. He gave Sun Tzu 180 imperial beauties and challenged Sun Tzu to train them to his strategic formation.

Sun Tzu divided the women into two troops, with two of the emperor's favorite concubines as their leaders. The emperor came to view the training display. Sun Tzu also ordered executioners to come to the site.

Sun Tzu gave the beauties instructions and a demonstration. He then signaled them to practice. Hearing the gongs, the ladies burst into laughter, and none of them followed his instructions. He said, "You have not understood my instructions. This is my responsibility." He then explained the movements all over again, but when the ladies heard the drums, they burst out laughing once more. He said sternly, "I have repeated my commands to you, yet you have not followed the orders. This is the leaders' responsibility." He then ordered the immediate execution of the emperor's two favorite concubines. Shocked, Emperor He Lu asked Sun Tzu to pardon them. Sun Tzu said, "They did not follow the commands. If they were to be pardoned, no one would obey you in the future." The two leaders were beheaded on the spot.

Sun Tzu appointed two other ladies as leaders and repeated the instructions. As soon as the drums sounded, the ladies made the precise movements and formations as instructed. Emperor He Lu was pleased with Sun Tzu and made him his army's commander in chief.

MODERN APPLICATIONS

SamSung Mobile Points at Apples while Scolding "Apple"

In the summer of 2012, I was entertained by the ad campaign that Samsung launched to highlight the differences between its Galaxy S III and the new Apple iPhone 5. Samsung used this clever stratagem to attack iPhone 5 indirectly: everything from the long queues at Apple stores to the smaller iPhone screen size, to file sharing. At the same time, Samsung backed up its campaign by advertising the Galaxy S III's powerful features. Using humor to balance the attack, Samsung never showed Apple logos or used Apple brand names, but, of course, everyone could identify exactly what Samsung was poking fun at. Focusing on comparing the features that customers really care about really made the campaign a success.

Kevin Bostic wrote on appleinsider.com that Samsung continued the momentum, taking Apple to task over *Iceland,* of all things! In an ad featuring balaclavas, goats, and apples, it attacked the iPhone for its language limitations, pointing out the iPhone's lack of voice-control support for the Icelandic language. Samsung's Galaxy S 4 supports the language, while Apple's Siri and dictation features cannot. The ad shows a man trying to use an actual apple in the way that one might handle an iPhone, but obviously with disappointing results. He hangs his head in frustration with the device, and a caption states, "Get a phone that understands you." I'll skip details of the ad and get to the end: the happy, smiling man taking a bite from an apple while holding a Galaxy mobile phone. By pointing at real apples, Samsung cleverly "scolded" Apple's features in its comparative ad.

The South China Sea: A Modern War

In 2005, eight Vietnamese fishermen were killed and eight others were detained by Chinese naval police. Many more detentions and more gunfire occurred later in the Gulf of Tonkin area. In March 2012, China detained twenty-one Vietnamese fishermen near the disputed Paracel islands in the South China Sea, accusing the men of fishing illegally in waters around the islands, which it has occupied since 1974. According to the BBC, China claims almost all this part of the South China Sea, an area rich in oil and other natural resources. At certain points, its territorial claims extend almost to the neighboring countries' coastlines, including those of the Philippines, Brunei, Malaysia, Vietnam, and Taiwan.

Also, since April 10, 2012, a Philippines naval vessel has been locked in a standoff with Chinese surveillance ships at the Scarborough Shoal, which both countries claim. Filipino and U.S. forces launched a fortnight of joint naval exercises in nearby seas. Later on, China sent a third patrol ship to reinforce the two already in the area. The dispute began when Manila accused Chinese fishermen of poaching in its waters.

China's killing and detention of fishermen from neighboring countries, and reinforcement of its naval presence sent the harshest intimidation and warning that it will claim sovereignty over the islands in the South China Sea at all costs.

IMPLEMENTATION TACTICS

Advertising

This stratagem is widely used in advertising. In a *Forbes* magazine article from September 20, 2012, John Ellett advises you run an ad criticizing your competition, without mentioning any names, but in such a clever way that consumers have no trouble drawing conclusions about the brand you are "scolding." The tactic is called *implicit comparison*. Samsung versus Apple, Dell versus Compaq, Procter and Gamble versus Unilever, and Baidu versus Google China nicely illustrate the stratagem of the clever indirect attack. To be effective, remember:

- Balance attack with humor to take off the edge of a competitive attack.

- Focus on the details of your product or service that solve the customer's pain and problems, while comparing these with what your competition *can't* provide.

Leadership and Management

Being indirect can be most effective whenever being direct could lead to problems such as bitterness, rebellion, or disruptive criticism. So use indirect means to get your way or to show what you mean or want. This can be useful for both disciplinary action and motivation. David Straker, founder of Changingminds.org, gives the first four of the following tips:

- Do not name names, so you cannot be accused. Use intermediaries, third parties and others.

- Cow the weak and convince the strong. Use scare tactics, threats, warnings and (even punishment).

- Make an example of those who do not comply with your commands or who oppose you. Use disproportionate punishment that will scare others into submission or bring them into line.

- Do not rely solely on extrinsic rewards to motivate your people. For example, pay them fairly, and then do everything you reasonably can to keep money out of their calculus for why they come to work. You do this by providing a sense of purpose, opportunity for growth and advancement, and desire to master their job.

- To get at the truth, pay attention to the nuances and subtleties, especially when interacting with Asian counterparts or companies.

- Always be aware that indirectness is a popular conflict resolution style in Asia.

Conflict Resolution

This strategy is the epitome of Asian-style indirect and collectivist culture in communication. "Pointing at the mulberry while scolding the locust tree" represents indirect conflict-resolution style. When dealing with indirect cultures, direct people need to remember:

- Always be mindful of "face." Keep face, give face and save face.

- Be sensitive to the importance of silence and deliberate pauses.

- Practice active listening skills.

- Use qualifiers, disclaimers, tag questions, and tentative statements.

- Be mindful that avoidance does not mean that the other party does not care. It is just used to avoid face-losing interaction—to maintain mutual face, dignity, and harmony.

When dealing with direct cultures, indirect people need to remember:

- Be mindful of problem-solving assumptions. Separate relationship from the problem.

- Learn to openly express opinions and points of view. One cannot rely entirely on nonverbal, intuitive understanding.

- Express with evidence, facts, and figures. Make a well-planned proposal.

- Be prepared for up-front challenge; accept criticism, counterproposals, and suggestions.

- Limit your use of silence since it can be taken for incompetence and inefficiency. Learn to ask more effective questions.

QUESTIONS TO CONSIDER

✓ *What action do you want your competition to take?*

✓ *How do you make a false attack to induce him to take that action?*

✓ *Whom do you want to influence?*

✓ *Which approach should you use when handling a conflict in your situation?*

✓ *How does your message make your prospects curious about your offering?*

Stratagem 27:
Feign Madness While Remaining Smart

Sometimes it is better to pretend to be foolish and take no action than to show off and rush into a situation recklessly. Be self-composed and plot secretly.

—The 36 Stratagems

LONG AGO IN CHINA

In A.D. 249, during the era of the Three Kingdoms, when the king of Wei died, the two loyal officials Sima Yi and Cao Shuang were charged with looking after the young prince Cao Fang, who was 8 years old. Cao Shuang took power from Shi by demanding complete control over the army. Sima Yi lived in fear that sooner or later, Cao Shuang would take his life as well. So he acted ill and weak in order to pose no threat to Cao Shuang. When one of Cao Shuang's henchmen came to visit, Sima Yi spilled soup on his robe and pretended to understand the conversation only vaguely. Sima Yi appeared as no threat and slipped off Cao Shuang's vigilance. Opportunity came when Cao Shuang took the young prince for a visit to the emperor's tomb. Sima Yi quickly gathered his men and family and staged a coup. Four days later, he had Cao Shuang executed and regained his power in Wei.

MODERN APPLICATIONS

Feign Ineptness to Beat the House

During the real estate bust starting in 2008, casinos in Las Vegas and Atlantic City, watching their revenues sink, were desperate for big spenders. Normally, every casino carefully categorizes high rollers according to how skillful they are at gambling. Some, who have the skills of a professional, could be banned from playing in the house.

Don Johnson was a big spender but was ranked as having only mediocre skills. To lure him into the house, casinos offered him fifty thousand dollars' worth of chips just to get him in for five days, hoping to employ the stratagem of "Toss out a brick to get a jade." The casinos' hard times meant a tremendous opportunity for Don. For one thing, fewer players meant that he was less likely to go up against highly skilled players. He just had to hone his skills and beat the dealer, that is, the "house." Also, since there weren't a lot of big spenders, and the casinos were desperate to get his business, Don could negotiate terms that put him in a more advantageous position. For example, he negotiated how the blackjack rules should be adjusted to accommodate him, and casinos gave him discounts as high as 20 percent. Thus, if he were to lose $600,000 at the Tropicana, he would have to pay only $480,000.

Don had accumulated almost two decades' experience playing blackjack. According to Alan Farnham and Susanna Kim on *ABC News,* March 21, 2012, along with having a gambling-related job as CEO of Heritage Development LLC, which develops computer-assisted wagering systems for horse racing, he teamed up with an Ivy League math PhD to analyze how he could improve his game and his odds and beat the house. By "feigning madness"—being classified as a mediocre player by the casino's ranking system—but "remaining smart" by creating all the right elements, he won $15 million from three Atlantic City casinos in five months during 2011. By now his prowess in blackjack has gotten him banned from all the major casinos. And yet, they pay him as a speaker to teach them how they can tighten up the weaknesses in their gambling system. He also attributed his winning tactics to his ability to be extremely disciplined and focused while using distraction to encourage the dealer to make mistakes.

The Columbo Interrogation Technique

Lieutenant Columbo, a Los Angeles detective played by Peter Falk in the 1970s television series *Columbo,* doesn't fit the cliché of an authoritarian lead detective. His rumpled attire and ambling gait give impression that he is far from being a professional. When he talks, his confused, bumbling demeanor further suggests incompetence, so that he is perceived as harmless. Every episode of the television program has a scene wherein Lt. Columbo is inspecting a crime scene and interviewing people associated with the victim. Unlike a typical policeman's gadfly manner, his friendliness and inconsequential chatter put people at ease and loosen their tongues, and before long, they are engaged in a distracting conversation.

He starts with casual open-ended questions, getting them to talk without reserve. When developing a bond by making the person relax, he slips in a question about what he really wants to know. Dave Straker, founder of changingminds.org, illustrates it this way: If Columbo wants to know whether a person drives a black car, he picks up a shade of black to start a false interrogation. Phrasing the question indirectly, he might start a conversation like this:

> "This is a nice clock. You know, I used to have a car
> exactly the same color as this. Chevy, it was."

> "Hey, I've got a black Chevy!"

> "Have you? Well, you know mine had a three
> twenty-seven with the four-barrel carb."

> "Well mine's a 'fifty-six. Special convertible!"

> "Not too many of those around."

> "Yeah. The guy down at the corner of Tenth Street gave
> me a good deal on it—needed the money bad."

And now the person has slipped his tongue without realizing that he has given the game away. The other trick that Columbo uses—again, when the other person's defenses are down, is that he begins to leave the scene, and is nearly out the door, when he stops and turns around to ask a question, which becomes his famous tag.

"Oh, ah, just one more thing—
is that your neighbor's car outside?"

The person being questioned has already reached closure on the session. Columbo's question thus catches him off guard and therefore he answers impulsively, just to complete closure. (According to Zeigarnick effect, the human mind is motivated to seek closure.)

By "feigning madness"—his rumpled look, bumbling demeanor, and inconsequential chatter—Lt. Columbo "remains smart" (tying together the entire investigation and establishing the suspect's culpability by using seemingly trivial and inconsequential details).

IMPLEMENTATION TACTICS

When the enemy has a low opinion of you,
encourage his arrogance even more.

—Sun Tzu

This stratagem advises you to avoid appearing to be a threat. When you appear nonthreatening, your adversary will discount you and your efforts. When they put their guard down, you will come in and attack. For Don, coming off as a high roller with low skills made the casinos even greedier for his money. They discounted him as a professional gambler. Meanwhile, he "remained smart," gathering all the tactics and expertise he needed—and broke the bank.

- Depending on the situation, pretend to be weak when you are actually strong. Thus, you avoid competition and lure your competitor into putting his guard down. Then you attack.

- Rather than talk, listen actively and ask effective questions so that you can gain information and exploit any slip of the tongue.

- Stay low key and avoid being a target.

Negotiation

- Leverage your strong position to renegotiate or change the rules of the game.

- Prepare, prepare, and then prepare some more.

- Be disciplined and mentally focused.

- Use the "Columbo technique" to tie unrelated details together.

QUESTIONS TO CONSIDER

✓ *What reaction from your competition do you need to prevent?*

✓ *What action do you need to take (How do you "feign madness"?) in order not to stir up competition?*

✓ *What do you need to work on so that you can strike when the opportunity arises?*

✓ *What practice exercises do you do to make sure you are perfect when engaging the customer?*

Stratagem 28:
Entice the Enemy onto the Roof, and Then Remove the Ladder

Expose your weaknesses purposely, enticing your enemy to penetrate your line. Then destroy him by surrounding him and cutting off his supply routes.

—The 36 Stratagems

LONG AGO IN CHINA

Han Xin, a well-known general, and his army were traveling to suppress two rebellions. When he reached the river Wei, a third kingdom sent out two hundred soldiers to try to stop him. He was faced with three options, none of them in his favor. He could attack the soldiers, but his men, wading through water to fight an enemy on solid terrain, would be at a tremendous disadvantage. He could withdraw, but he may lose his life for failing to accomplish the mission. Or he could wait, but then his enemy would hold him back from moving forward on time.

He ordered his men to dam the river upstream with sandbags. By the next morning, the river had diminished to a trickle, and his soldiers could easily cross. Soon after the two armies engaged, Han Xin ordered his men to retreat. His enemy, wanting to conquer, followed them onto the riverbed. When half the opposing army had crossed the shallow river, he ordered another troop of his men, hiding behind the dam, to dismantle the barrier. A wall of water crashed down, drowning those who were crossing the river.

MODERN APPLICATIONS

The Canali Suit

I was working in my office when my husband dragged me to the Nordstrom store with him, telling me that Dosi had just called to say Nordstrom was offering a 30 percent discount for men. We fought the Christmas traffic to see Dosi, my husband's favorite salesgirl at Nordstrom, who was all smiles, serving four other customers. She told us to shop around and come back to see her in thirty minutes. So there we were, bored and mindlessly spending money on things that we didn't need, just to kill some time. When we came back, Dosi ushered us into the glamorous Canali section. She said, "I've been eyeing this suit for you. It's rare, and you have the right build for it—this tailored Italian cut is not for everybody, you know." We were concerned looking at the price tag of $1,899 before tax, but Dosi pointed out what a difference the 30 percent discount would make. "Just try them on to see how they hang on you," she said. My husband tried them on, and the exquisite fabric made him look like a perfect V-shaped David Beckham. Before we knew it, we had to buy a $170 Canali tie to go with it and have the sleeve buttons costumed the Italian way for an extra $64. And then, of course, "Oh, by the way, a Canali blue blazer is timeless. How about a couple of pairs of Canali pants to switch around with the blazer since it could go with any color?"

Dosi had cleverly and gradually "enticed us to the roof" by offering the special 30 percent off, then "encircled" us in the Nordstrom department to buy needless things, then "removed the ladder" when we were committed to buying the pricey suit. At this point, we were trapped with a huge money commitment (no escape route), so any other additional charges and expenses would seem insignificant (because psychologically we feel obliged to act consistently with the internal explanation we have built—the reason why we bought the suit to begin with.)

The Beauty Industry

Aesthetic filler products are available not only at beauty salons but also at all kinds of clinics such as tattoo removal salons, dental offices, and spas. In a sluggish economy, the consumption of Botox, a highly purified form of botulinum bacterium toxin that paralyzes muscle, thereby ironing out wrinkles, is rising at a double-digit clip. Allergan is the best-known company for producing aesthetic filler products, including Botox, Juvéderm, and breast implants. While Allergan also produces drugs that treat serious medical conditions, fully one-third of its sales come from the high-growth products, ringing up $1.8 billion in sales for 2012. This is a lucrative business because the customer needs "refilling" every three to six months, on average. Small clinics or beauty salons offer a free try of Botox on one small area of the face to "entice" the customer "onto the roof." Once one area of the face gets the Botox injection, chances are good that the customer will come back to get her whole face done or at least to get that area refilled. Dr Carter Singh, at Derbyshire Royal Infirmary, said, "It is easy to see how people could become addicted." One of the regular customers said, "Once you start having Botox, it's very hard to stop, as you get used to the way your face looks. I'm terrified that if I stop now, all my frown lines and wrinkles will return."

Trapped in a Time-Share Scheme

My first trip to Las Vegas, in 2000, was an amazing experience. I got offers of free tickets to a musical show, and four free nights at the Bellagio just for being willing to take a half-day tour to this very nice resort area. It was not a bad deal: giving up half my day for such nice freebies.

Before I knew it, they had taken us to this place and made us sit through a long sales presentation for their time-share properties. The salespeople used various sales techniques: conveying a sense of urgency ("sign up now to get a 35 percent discount—today only"); social proof ("this place was resided in by such-and-such famous person in the entertainment industry"); a sense of scarcity ("only a few blocks available"); a sense of achievement ("why not reward yourself for your hard work?"). And amazingly, I watched people still falling for the same old buying pressure and emotional sales tactics. My brother-in-law Matt, who can be pretty gullible, was one of them. Coming back from the trip, when reality set in, he changed his mind, had to go through a lot of headache and dispute, and ended up losing the five thousand dollars' deposit.

IMPLEMENTATION TACTICS

In this stratagem, the "ladder" is the escape route. After being lured to the "roof," and with the escape route shut down, your enemy fights with all his might, eventually exhausting himself because he had to fight in your stronghold. More broadly, you can create a situation that forces the actions you desire.

Sales and Marketing

This stratagem uses a freebie as the bait to lure the prospect up the "ladder." Once they are up there, the ladder is removed— the salespeople use various tactics to lure the prospect to a spontaneous buying decision. The stratagem can take many guises:

- loyalty programs, bonus cards, points, customer cards
- freebies and other gimmicks
- up-sale, cross-sale, peer pressure
- easy installment plan if a prospect can't or won't pay in full

Negotiation

In negotiation, put your counterpart in a "fait accompli" situation: everything has been set up and done, and you then apologize (preferably with a plausible reason) for doing it. Remember:

- Encourage your counterpart to make bold public commitments, where going against these would cause a loss of face and status.

Leading and Managing Change

- Facilitate a small change in one specific behavior; then use it to transform habit and culture.

- Create small, fast "wins" to motivate people to follow through, to achieve the bigger goal.

- When setting a goal, have an accountability partner, or declare it in public. This is how you drive for success: by "removing the ladder" so that you can't back out on your words.

QUESTIONS TO CONSIDER

✓ *What is your plan for upselling your customer?*

✓ *What is you strategy to cross-sell your current customer?*

✓ *How do you plan to ask your customer for an introduction to another business?*

✓ *How can you make it easier for your customer to do business with you?*

✓ *How do you entice your customer to take the first action?*

✓ *What do you do to get your customer committed to your product or service?*

✓ *How do encourage your people to take the initiative?*

✓ *What do you do to keep your people committed to the change?*

Stratagem 29:
Deck the Tree with False Blossoms

Create a deceptive appearance to make your battle array appear stronger than it is. Just as with the flock of wild geese soaring across the sky— the grandeur of their flying formation is greatly enhanced by the display of their extended wings.

—The 36 Stratagems

LONG AGO IN CHINA

In A.D. 420, the Bei Wei soldiers attacked the town of Ji Nan. The two armies fought over thirty battles in twenty days. The Song army won all the battles and chased the enemy all the way to the city of Li. General Tan of the Song was a very able man who grew arrogant from the continual victories, though he remained vigilant against his enemy's ambush. The Bei Wei army tricked the Song army, however, and set fire to their food supply.

A turncoat from the Song army ran to the Bei Wei to report the Song's dire reality. Learning this, the Bei Wei army decided to launch a fierce battle to vanquish the Song.

At night, the Song's camp was well lit, and General Tan and a few men were counting many bags of white grains in the warehouses. The rumor traveled to the Bei Wei that the Song had been aided with lots of food supplies. Little did they know that Tan had ordered his men to fill the sacks with white sand and cover it with a thin layer of rice on top. The Bei Wei, who had been defeated by the Song army several times before, withdrew without launching an attack. The next day, they donned their armor and paraded on the street without being confronted by the opposing army. They escaped safely back to their fortified city.

MODERN APPLICATIONS

The Art of Packaging

It was a surprisingly chilly day in November 2012 in South Beach Miami. My best friends and I discovered the Setai Hotel restaurant. As soon as we walked in, we were welcomed by the pleasant warmth from the open fire of the tandoori kitchen, where we could see and talk to the young Asian chef throwing his naan dough in the air. All around us was a visual feast: bright yellow turmeric, red peppercorns, Peking duck turning in the glass oven. We looked at each other. This was it. We settled at a table near the fire to enjoy the fine trans-Asian cuisine. The place regularly hosts such celebrities as Madonna, Heidi Klum, and Sheryl Crow. What makes it different? What makes the place attract these celebrities and fill its rooms that begin at eight hundred dollars a night? The teak paneling and the antique bricks from Shanghai, the rustic wine cellar, antique Chinese artworks on the wall—all this decor makes the experience uniquely Asian in the heart of bustling South Beach Miami.

According to *Fortune* magazine (July 22, 2013), Chrysler TV ads are all about the American story. One is about returning war veterans, narrated by Oprah Winfrey, and another is about farmers, featuring Paul Harvey as the voice of God. And these ads, which convey such a sense of Americana and patriotism, come from a foreign-owned company. Exor is a Fortune 500 investment company headquartered in Turin, Italy. Besides owning Chrysler and 30 percent of Fiat, Exor owns Ferrari, Maserati, Lancia, and Alfa Romeo and has big holdings in commercial real estate brokerage, banking, media, and the Turin soccer team Juventus. Ten years ago, three-quarters of Exor's revenues came from

Europe; today Europe accounts for less than one-third. Exor's biggest market now is the United States. Exor is smart to craft a message resonating with the market where it reaps the most profit.

After buying a jar of sauce that looked as if its tomatoes had been handpicked in Italy and processed by local Sicilians, I was excited to prepare a rustic Italian meal for my family. While waiting for the sauce to simmer on the stove, I carefully looked at the jar from all angles. And there I found it, at the bottom of the jar, in tiny fancy cursive font that could pass for calligraphy: "*A product of Unilever.*"

Multilevel and Direct-Sales Firms "Deck with False Blossoms"

I have been invited to two Pampered Chef cookware parties by two different neighbors, a Mary Kay cosmetics get-together by one of my colleagues, fashion clothing trunk sales by friends, and an Herbalife sample party by my son's teacher. I can't remember how many times friends and acquaintances have tried to recruit me for their "downlines." And every time, I feel obligated to make a purchase, as if I owed it to the relationship we have as friends, colleagues, family, or neighbors. I wonder how this direct-sales system sustains itself, because at the end of the day, a direct seller will necessarily run out of friends, colleagues, neighbors, and family. And when they try to recruit their own customers, the customers-friends-family-neighbors now become their direct competition.

Believe it or not, direct selling, whether it's gourmet food, cosmetics, or insurance, is a $30 billion industry in the United States, and a $17 billion industry (2008) in China. Kim, an old colleague of mine, quit her job and joined forces with her husband to work full-time as a Nu Skin distributor. They worked very hard and moved up to become regional managers, sales superstars, and world leaders, winning all kinds of glory and awards. While attempting to recruit me, Kim passionately painted how the "Nu Skin family" has changed her life for the better, given her a grip on leadership, and enabled her to design her own destiny. Kim is actually a rare success story among the many other cases of people I know who ended up stocking a boatload of samples in their house and quitting. I was once invited to teach leadership skills for a small multilevel marketing (MLM) firm. I have learned that there are legitimate and bogus MLM firms, and those who blur the gray line in between.

Here's how they earn money. Direct sellers, or "consultants," market their products in a variety of ways, including one-on-ones, home parties, trunk shows, and the Internet. The seller is compensated for her own product sales as well as a piece of the sales of her recruits and her recruits' recruits. That is why bad MLM firms are referred to as "pyramid" schemes. In addition to paying sales commissions, many multilevel marketing firms offer their agents the possibility of scoring free trips, bonuses, and special rewards. "Caveat emptor" applies, though—not all direct-sales companies are honest and aboveboard, and pyramid schemes and other bogus "opportunities" are common.

Illegal MLM firms to watch out for include direct-selling revenues that depend exclusively on recruiting people instead of selling products. Other warning signs are recruiters who won't share details of the compensation plan; who make a newly recruited seller invest heavily in product samples, training, and marketing packages; and who offer no buyback plan or inventory return policy. The thing is, it's not easy to spot a pyramid scheme. A lot of companies use actual products and a sophisticated disguise to appear legitimate when they are, in essence, just another pyramid racket.

Regardless, the direct-sales business model is the best illustration of the stratagem "Deck the tree with false blossoms." A "bare tree," which is the company that has nothing or, at most, an iffy product line, keeps on "decking" with layers of recruited sellers, or downline. It is troublesome when the sellers at all levels (the downline) are actually the consumers. According to Joel Rosenblatt in *Bloomberg Businessweek* (December 6, 2013), Herbalife has been under scrutiny amid allegations by hedge-fund manager Bill

Ackman that the company is a pyramid scheme. According to CNBC.com (Jan 16, 2014), China had ordered an investigation into Nu Skin. The move comes a day after the People's Daily published a story accusing the company of exaggerating its influence and organizing "brainwashing" gatherings.

Ponzi schemes and pyramid scheme use this stratagem, in the literal translation, to the fullest. My mother's neighbor, Lara, called, telling her to invest in a shopping plaza development project in California, at a return on investment of 20 percent. She pulled up the laptop, pointing at a grandiose Web site with nice blueprints of strip mall development projects. My mom was sucked into it until I did some educational analysis of the current economy for her. Bank interest rates were at an all-time low, so why on earth would the company pay investors many times what it would have to pay the bank? Six months later, Lara told my mom that she lost $5,000, and her friend who recruited her lost $15,000—actually, only $14,300, because he earned $700 for recruiting Lara. The Web site was pulled, and the toll-free number turned out to be bogus.

IMPLEMENTATION TACTICS

> Water is fluid, yet it can take any shape and cut
> through everything. In warfare, he who can adapt his
> tactics to his enemy's situation thereby succeeds.
>
> —Sun Tzu

A tree generally bears no colorful flowers, but if "decked with false blossoms," it can look like something it is not. This stratagem advocates forming a network that can become stronger than parts. A second meaning concerns using the right materials to enhance your position and adapt to the situation. One word of caution: beware of those who deck a "bare tree" with false blossoms—using splendid materials to embellish a wretched reality such as a Ponzi or pyramid scheme.

Marketing

- Package and create perception in your favor to make you or your product/services appear in the best possible light.

- Build brand and credibility.

- Create the right image in your favor.

- To be promoted, market yourself by projecting your potential. You are promoted not for your performance in your current position but for the perceived potential of performing at the next level.

Business Communication

Although perception is not reality, it *is* reality to the perceiver. Thus, you can manage perceptions to manage a person's reality.

- Polish communication skills such as choice of words, delivery of a message, and tone.

- Project the right image through gesture, attitude, and style.

- Dress for success.

- "Dress not for who you are but for who you want to be." —Chin Ning Chu

Business Expansion

Power is not just the real potential you have; it is the perception of, and assumptions about, your power that others hold. Understand the difference between power you actually have, power that you believe you have, and power that others think you have. Identify the gaps, and never mistake one for another.

- Form alliances, organize associations, or join existing associations to create a strong, consolidated front and network.

- Attract partners, alliances, and contributors to form a strong force.

QUESTIONS TO CONSIDER

✓ *How can you appear to be larger then you really are?*

✓ *Does you wardrobe give the right image for your business environment?*

✓ *Does your communication effectively describe your business?*

✓ *Does you language create the images that compel favorable responses?*

✓ *Are you conducting your networking activities in the right place to meet the people you need to meet?*

✓ *What actions are you taking to attract partners or build strong alliances?*

✓ *What actions must you take to induce them to cooperate?*

> ## Stratagem 30:
> ## Make the Guest Become the Host
>
> *Try to put a foot through the crack in the door. Control the brain of your enemy by gradually entering into his body and exerting influence. Eventually, you will take full control.*
>
> —The 36 Stratagems

LONG AGO IN CHINA

When Xiang Liang's home state of Chu fell to the power of the Qin dynasty, Xiang Liang fled with his nephew, Xiang Yu, and took asylum in the state of Wu.

Xiang Liang developed a reputation as a strong leader, built trust and credibility, and slowly climbed up the organizational ladder until he was assigned a post as a well-respected adviser for the Wu administration.

In 209 B.C., when states and kingdoms throughout the Qin dynasty rebelled, the governor of Wu asked Xiang Liang to lead his army to join the rebellion. Xiang Liang and his nephew, Xiang Yu, accepted the challenge and requested a meeting to strategize about the revolution plan. In the middle of the meeting, on Xiang Liang's signal, Xiang Yu withdrew his sword and beheaded the governor. Xiang Liang declared himself governor and immediately killed any objecting witnesses.

MODERN APPLICATIONS:

Hyundai: From Apprentice to Builder of the National Car

Richard M. Steers wrote in his book *Made in Korea* that in 1968, Ford Motor Company agreed to have Hyundai become an assembler of Ford Cortinas. It allowed Hyundai to use Korean parts and materials as much as possible and also agreed to provide technical assistance to the Korean auto-parts industry. Ford engineers taught Hyundai the business from start to finish, including planning, scheduling, product assembly, inspection, and quality control. After the first two years, the two companies began discussing a joint venture, but the plan never materialized, because both sides fought for management control. First, Hyundai proposed to make Hyundai-built Fords, to be sold throughout Ford's global distribution channel, but Ford rejected the idea. Instead, Ford suggested that Hyundai participate in making cars using Ford-designed engines with Australian-made chassis and Japanese-made transmissions. Insulted, Chung immediately set about finding alternative routes to realizing his dream of becoming a global automaker. To learn about how the entire industry worked from the ground up, he sent experts to Australia to study production technologies, to Japan to study after-sales service, and to the United States to learn marketing and distribution systems. Even though Hyundai continued to assemble Ford Cortinas for several more years, Chung's heart was not in the venture.

Sensing that the joint-venture relationship was deteriorating, while recognizing that Hyundai still needed foreign supplies and technical assistance, Chung approached General Motors, Volkswagen, and Alfa Romeo. But he fared no better, because no one offered the management control and independence that Hyundai wanted. Finally, Chung approached Mitsubishi, and both parties achieved what they were looking for. At the time, Mitsubishi was desperately competing with larger Japanese firms such as Toyota and Nissan while striving to increase its market share. Hyundai could have complete management control and build its own nameplate cars, using technical designs from Japan for everything from engines to transmissions. Fueled by the Korean president's directives urging Korean carmakers to build a "national car," Chung set out for Europe to search for design assistance. First, he met with ItalDesign, a stylist company for Alfa Romeo and Fiat. Then he met with George Turnbull, a former president of British Leyland. He hired Turnbull immediately to be vice president of Hyundai Motor Company. Turnbull's contribution was invaluable in making Chung's vision a reality. By 1976, the new plant was completed, and the new model, the Pony—Korean's first national car—came online.

Foreign-Invested Pharmaceutical Companies in China

China has long treated foreign companies as a source of capital, technology, and managerial know-how as it builds its own economy up to a global scale. For a long time, China has offered low tax rates, inexpensive land, and other incentives to foreign enterprises while wooing them into joint ventures with local partners. Now that China's own industries have matured and the country is well capitalized, it can crack the whip on foreign enterprises without worrying about upsetting them. According to Dexter Roberts and Carol Matlack in *Bloomberg Businessweek* (September 19, 2013), in late July 2013, China fired a warning shot for foreign businesses targeting its pharmaceutical market, indicating that China would not "let foreign companies as guests take over China" and that the Chinese are in charge.

China's National Development and Reform Commission has led a crackdown to investigate European and U.S multinationals for anticompetitive behavior. GlaxoSmithKline, along with Bayer, Eli Lilly, and many others, is being investigated for alleged corrupt practices and price fixing. Danone's baby-formula maker, Dumex, formerly punished for price fixing, is facing claims that it paid "sponsorship fees" to bribe staff at hospitals in Tianjin to sell its baby formula. Some companies have bribed doctors and hospital administrators to prescribe their drugs. Some have hired private investigators to find out the critical business elements, including what connections to officials a Chinese partner may have, whether the partner's finances are adequate, and how to make connections with persons of influence. In August 2013, Peter Humphrey, a British citizen, who had worked as an investigator for Glaxo, was arrested and jailed, along with his wife.

IMPLEMENTATION TACTICS

The stratagem advises accepting an inferior position so that you don't appear as a threat—getting a foot in the door and then extending your influence beyond the immediate arena when your rival isn't watching. Lenovo, Microsoft, and Intel, for instance, all began in an inferior position to IBM and built up power from there. Hyundai started as an apprentice to Ford, and a distributor for Mitsubishi. The stratagem also suggests that one should exploit opportunity to move from a passive to an active position. Wee Chow-Hou and Lan Luh Luh advise in the book *The 36 Strategies of the Chinese* that many steps are involved in switching from "guest" to "host." First, one must be welcome and trusted as a guest. Then, as a guest, one should not arouse suspicion. All the while, the guest must be alert, to seize the opportunity the moment it arises. (For example, when the governor of Wu invited his guest Xiang Liang to help plot the revolution, Xiang Liang saw and seized the opportunity.) Then the guest leverages this opportunity to expand his influence. He must wrestle for full control and take over the host. Finally, once becoming the host, he needs to consolidate his power so that he won't be removed.

- Joint-venture to learn the ropes; then take over, buy out, or establish on your own.

- Develop trust and credibility.

- Make them (competition or customer or partner) dependent on you.

- Take charge of needed resources; gradually assume control over desired access to people and things.

- Become an expert, the "go-to" person. If you are indispensable, people must come to you for advice and knowledge.

- Be cautious of being taken over by *your* guest.

QUESTIONS TO CONSIDER

✓ *What inferior position can you take now to allay your competition's suspicions so that they discount you as a threat?*

✓ *Identify the levers you need to build to establish your influence and control over your competition.*

✓ *What is your plan of execution to acquire those levers?*

✓ *What step do you need to consider to strengthen your alliances?*

✓ *How do you consolidate power to avoid being taken over?*

CHAPTER 6

Desperate Stratagems

Stratagem 31:
Use a Woman to Ensnare a Man
(the Beauty Trap)

When faced with a strong enemy, try to tame its leader. When dealing with a resourceful leader, try to take down his morale. Exploit his indulgence in sexual pleasure to cripple his fighting spirit. When his fighting spirit falters, his men's morale will shatter and their force will be greatly weakened. To conserve your strength, take advantage of your enemy's weakness.

—The 36 Stratagems

Long Ago in China

During the Spring and Autumn period, the States of Wu and Yue were constantly at war. Fu Chai, the king of Wu, was almost unapproachable, for he was surrounded by a skilled and watchful entourage. Fan Li, a clever adviser for the Yue, thought of a scheme to break through the protection surrounding Fu Chai.

He found Xi Shi, a beautiful young girl, and trained her to dance, recite poetry, and paint. When Xi Shi turned 16, she was sent to serve Fu Chai, who was mesmerized by her beauty and talent. Her mission was to ensnare Fu Chai and turn him and his right-hand man against each other. Her ravishing beauty made the task easy. King Fu Chai lost interest in running his kingdom and kept missing meetings. Xi Shi plotted to make King Fu Chai suspect his right-hand man's loyalty. Eventually, for his own peace of mind, Fu Chai had his right-hand man beheaded. One day, seizing the opportunity when Fu Chai left his home base, the army of Yue, with its allies, attacked and conquered the kingdom of Wu.

MODERN APPLICATIONS

The Wild Woman of Wall Street and Her Way to Wealth

As we saw in the discussion of stratagem five, Lynn Tilton, a self-made billionaire businesswoman, is the founder and CEO of Patriarch Partners, a private-equity firm that specializes in taking over distressed manufacturers in male-dominated industries. Her acquisitions include MD helicopters, fire-truck maker American LaFrance, and automotive systems manufacturer Dura. She caught my attention when she showed up for an interview with Barbara Walters in a low-cut top, supershort miniskirt, and stiletto heels. "Most women feel they need to be more like men to be successful," says Tilton. "I believe that women should be women."

She developed a relentless work ethic at a young age. She started her homework at four a.m. and practiced tennis after school until it was dark, becoming a tennis star in high school. After graduating from Yale, she took a job at Morgan Stanley. She got married, had a child, divorced and returned to Wall Street, got her MBA at Columbia in fourteen months, and soon found herself working at Goldman Sachs. She spent two decades working in that male-dominated environment and left the last investment firm, Amroc, as a partner in 1998, with ten million in the bank. Back in the late 1980s, Wall Street was not the friendliest work environment for women. "It was a very difficult place to balance striving in a man's world and being a woman," she says. "You either got comfortable or you left." In 1991, she sued Merrill Lynch for sexual harassment. Due to the terms of the settlement, not much detail is available.Tilton is known for putting a man in his place when necessary, and yet, she is also known for being flirty. In 1998, she sent her top former clients a raunchy Christmas card. It featured two pictures: one of her in a red lace bodysuit and Santa hat and straddling a stepladder, and the other of her in black lingerie and high boots, wielding a whip. (You can easily find those legendary images on the Web.)

"I spent most of my career listening to men ask me what I was wearing and what color my underwear was," she says, "so that was my farewell gift. I was an attractive woman in an industry with few women. It was a joke to those men."

In a *Forbes* magazine article from April 17, 2011, Jenna Goudreau says that Tilton played the sex-kitten card during the mid-1990s when she worked on the sales and trading desk of Amroc Investments. According to Goudreau, several former employees, who declined to be named because they're afraid of being sued, say that Tilton (51 years old in 2011), uses her "woman-ness"—her sexuality—as a blunt instrument.

In an interview with Jessica Pressler of *New York* magazine on April 10, 2011, Tom Bernard, Tilton's colleague at that time, says, "She liked to be provocative. "Sometimes you'd walk by and hear her on the phone and be like, 'Hmmm.'" She is known for her flirtatious style and provocative attire. Regardless, most of her former employees praised her for her work ethic, business acumen, and compelling leadership style. The most important thing they say is that she has strong convictions and that she cares. By all accounts, Tilton is a sharp, savvy businesswoman. Around late 2000, when the economy tanked, she and her business partner purchased a portfolio of distressed commercial loans at a 26 percent discount and packaged them using Ark, a collateralized-loan obligation structure that Tilton later patented. "She's definitely very bright, has great command of the issues that she's been working on, and her motivations are extraordinarily public-spirited," says Richard Levin, president of Yale University.

Stephen Gray, a managing partner at the crisis management firm CRG Partners, has worked with Tilton for the past five years. "She dresses in ways that are extreme for a room full of bankers," he says. "She tries to distract them from the deal."

"Do I like to take people off balance?" Tilton asks. "Yeah. Once people are off balance, they listen."

Her provocative style and refusal to look and act according to business conventions is strategically a tactic to gain the upper hand. By using her "woman-ness", Tilton distracts the competition or counterpart from the deal, "ensnaring" them to her advantage. Meanwhile, she is fully aware that exploiting her sexuality could backfire and that her style could overshadow her substance. Still, according to her, she wants to provide the whole package: savvy business sense, entertainment value, and a fascinating personality.

Implementation Tactics

> *Know yourself and your enemy.*
> *One hundred battles, one hundred wins.*
>
> —Sun Tzu

While the literal application of this stratagem is to use beauty and sexual desire to ensnare, corrupt, or distract the enemy, in a broader sense it also implies unseating your rival by providing something that he desires and needs. By satisfying those desires and needs, you can distract and manipulate him. This is best applied as a distraction to lure the target's attention away from what should be the main concerns. In the first stratagem, "Deceive heaven to cross the sea," distractions can take many forms, from creating a diverting environment to appealing to emotions or to the desire for self-esteem, social status, or trust. The "beauty trap" stratagem appeals to human desires for sex, beauty, and youthfulness. Going back into prehistory, cave paintings often portrayed sex scenes. Tens of thousands of years later, ancient Rome's public art was filled with sexual content. Ancient Chinese and feudal Japanese artists were no less inspired by sexual in their artwork. In every period of history, sex has been used as an effective weapon. And today, the art of business entertainment, especially in Asia, is not complete without beautiful women. A sophisticated host understands and provides for the desires of the guests. In an ambience of alcohol and lovely women—the distractions—the barriers between parties in a business relationship become blurry. When one loses vigilance and puts his guard down, the other strikes and "ensnares" him for her or her employers' purposes. Remember:

- Identify what your counterpart or competition needs and wants.

- Identify your levers and how you can move them to achieve your end goal.

Makers of beer, wine, cosmetics, and cigarettes regularly hire attractive women to promote or endorse their products. Asian airline companies and the fashion industry also use the "beauty trap" stratagem to good effect.

Shaping Perception

- Use attractive appearance as an asset.

- Shape perception to your advantage.

- Polish the appearance, build a favorable image, and sharpen communication skills to your advantage. Remember, perception is reality.

- For better odds of success, form a complete package of attractive appearance, pleasant attitude, and high performance.

Gaining a Competitive Edge in a Corrupt Marketplace

In examining uses of the beauty trap in business, we must be quite clear about corruption and what it means to cross that line. To get a foothold in a market (especially Asian markets), an individual or organization can be tempted to resort to bribery. Corruption exists everywhere, of course, differing only in kind and degree from place to place. And operating in some markets rife with corruption poses frustration and also danger. While bribery is never to be condoned, companies must have a deep understanding of the situation if they intend to survive, let alone prosper. Companies that survive the experience and learn from it can develop a powerful competitive edge over their competition. Here are a few suggestions when operating in a corrupt business environment:

- *Understand* the rules: Find out the extent of corruption in the market, and the "culture" of doing business in a country. Examine closely your company's stand on this. For example, how does your company define the words "gift" and "bribe"? What is the monetary limit beyond which a gift becomes something more? Where is the cutoff line? And be especially aware of your own country's laws regarding bribery. For example, it is illegal for a U.S. company to bribe foreign officials, even if the entire transaction happens in another country.

- *Explore* and provide alternatives: Be creative! Instead of outright payments, companies can provide ethically appropriate incentives such as sponsoring professional training programs and professional symposiums; heading up movements to develop grassroots talents; providing equipment and technology for an organization; or funding an R & D project, scholarship, or sports event.

Here are some suggestions by Roberto Martin N. Galang (John Gokongwei School of Management, Ateneo de Manila University), in his book *Doing Business in Corrupt Places:*

- *Establish* political influence. Lobby governments to reduce overall red tape and corruption, and ally with other companies to argue for more reasonable regulatory rules or to alter a regulation in your favor.

- *Ally* with your competitors in the industry to create a self-regulating industry association, which helps shift the power from government bureaucrats to the industry and its stakeholders.

- *Joint-venture* with state-owned enterprises or local firms. Get influential stakeholders on your side to influence political decision makers and reduce the risk of regulatory interference.

- *Escape* is sometimes the best strategy. If the situation is too arduous or too risky, accept the bureaucratic delays or walk away. Avoid the market for now and wait for the right conditions to strike back.

QUESTIONS TO CONSIDER

✓ *What is your product or service's unique appeal?*

✓ *What is your product or service's "sex appeal"?*

✓ *What does your competition desire?*

✓ *How can you satisfy your counterpart's desire, and what can you expect to get out of that?*

Stratagem 32:
The Open-City Scheme

At times, it is better to display deliberately your weakness to confuse the enemy so that he is puzzled or tricked into putting his guard down. When your force is desperately inferior to your enemy's, this stratagem can turn the tide.

—The 36 Stratagems

LONG AGO IN CHINA

During the Three Kingdoms period, Kung Men sent most of his troops off to battle, leaving his city without an army to protect it. Unfortunately, his enemy Si Ma, the general of Wei, made an unexpected approach with 150,000 soldiers while Kung Men had only 2,500 troops to protect the city.

Realizing that the Wei army outnumbered his by sixty to one, he could neither fight nor escape. After making his soldiers dress as civilians, Kung Men sent an old man to open the city's entrance gate. Then he went up to his tower, to play the zither and recite poetry while servants brought him food and wine. General Si Ma's spies came back and reported that the city gates were open, civilians were calmly sweeping the streets, and Kung Men was playing serene songs. This obviously carefree attitude confused Si Ma. The strange atmosphere of calm in an open city made him suspect a cunning trap. So he ordered his troops to retreat and wait until he could find out what was really going on inside the city. While Si Ma hesitated to take action, Kung Men's men returned home from their campaign in time to defend their city.

MODERN APPLICATIONS:

Google "Opens the Gates" to Confuse Bill Gates

According to David A. Vise's book *The Google Story,* Bill Gates was poking around on the Google Web site in December 2003 and came across a job ad with descriptions of all the job openings at Google. He was surprised to see that a search company was posting job notices for engineers trained in operating-system design, distributed-systems architecture, and other areas that were more in Microsoft's areas of expertise than in Google's. The next day, he sent a notice warning top Microsoft executives to watch the Google guys, since they appeared to be planning an assault on Microsoft that was much bigger than merely a battle of search engines.

Meanwhile, Google used the open-city scheme to unveil a list of new products ranging from G-mail to search via mobile phone. Google did not make a focused onslaught against Microsoft Desktop, but it confused Microsoft and used that confusion to good effect.

Although Microsoft failed to impress users with its Bing search engine, it still had a virtual monopoly with its operating system controlling the personal computer desktop. And it was determined to pick up millions of global users by developing a built-in search engine that would be the thrust in front of users every time they turned on their PC. But even Microsoft's abundant resources did not guarantee victory. For even though the company had recruited an army of skilled software engineers, it hadn't been able to attract experts in the specialized field of *search.* Desperately fighting on the search front while defending against an assault on its operating system, giant Microsoft went sprawling.

In 2006, in another deft use of the open-city scheme, Google unveiled Google Docs (now Google Drive). One of my editors used Google Docs, which allowed us to collaborate and edit documents in real time. Documents can be shared, opened, and edited by multiple users simultaneously. Unlike Microsoft which perfected its products and would not launch them until they were flawless, Google "opened the gates" to solicit feedback and responses from users and competition by introducing its products when they were still at early stages of development. They are cool, free services that have room for improvement. Users don't pay for them, so they don't complain if products are not fully developed. On the contrary, users are seriously involved and eager to contribute feedback, so Google can shorten its learning curve and churn out more and better free products. In openly displaying its room for improvement, Google's bypassing and marginalizing of Windows and other Microsoft software started to seep in as a reality. In fact, users can adopt Google's free services, regardless of its flaws, and become much less dependent on Microsoft software. Today, we can write, post, edit, and print documents without using Windows—Microsoft's bread and butter.

By applying the open-city scheme, Google confused and tired out Microsoft, the once invincible giant that steamrolled over every rival in its path.

Revealing Weaknesses and Vulnerabilities

As a public speaker, I find that my audiences are most engaged and connected when they hear about my struggles, failures, and setbacks and how I emerge and rise above the circumstances. This could seem counterintuitive. After all, you would think that audiences come to hear successful people share all about their glorious achievements. But the fact is, my speaking audiences couldn't care less about my achievements. They want to hear how I *fail*—how I pick myself up and overcome adversity. Over the years, I have rewritten my materials, letting the introducer present my credentials and give more room for me to share my vulnerability and humility.

Recently, I gave the keynote address at a conference to a group of litigation attorneys and executives. You might think that in such a male-dominated, testosterone-driven environment, I would have a tougher time relating to the audience if I didn't emphasize winning and defeating the competition. But I was pleasantly surprised. By "opening the city"—sharing and talking about weaknesses as well as strengths—I could inspire them to embrace uncertainty and setbacks.

When I finished my speech, one of the executives came up to me and told me I had started their yearly educational conference on the perfect note. Moreover, he said that I made him and his people stretch beyond their normal ways of thinking and inspired them to be authentic leaders in their organizations.

IMPLEMENTATION TACTICS

Though the enemy is stronger in numbers,
we may prevent him from fighting.

—Sun Tzu

This stratagem literally advises purposely exposing "fullness" or "emptiness" and using the display to lead the adversary in a certain direction. Ponzi schemes, the use of bogus companies, and confidence games are literal applications of the stratagem where winning is a zero-sum game. In a business competition, your competitors watch and study your every step, trying to anticipate your moves and where you might pose a threat. We are accustomed to keeping information as hidden as possible. This stratagem, on the other hand, suggests unorthodox thinking. Rather than hide, you can strategically reveal your information to shape and influence your competitor's assessment and reaction to your own advantage.

Google openly revealed to Microsoft its unfinished products, and it threw Microsoft's headhunters into a tizzy by publicly recruiting for positions that implied dangerous designs. By purposely opening up its world, Google confused Microsoft and forced it to fight on multiple fronts, thereby wearing down its spirit and resources. Secondly, by being open with users about its room for improvement, Google has expanded its global community. You, too, can use the "open city":

- Create mystery and confusion with a deliberate display of your weaknesses.

- Get people involved in building trust and relationships because, psychologically, people want to build, fix, contribute, and be a part of some important cause.

Influential Leadership

Deep down inside, we all are well aware of the chinks in our own armor. If a leader of a team or organization has the courage to admit that she is not flawless, that she messes up and then learns from it, she will open up a new environment of trusting, learning, and encouraging her people to take more calculated risks. Openly revealing vulnerabilities does not undercut a leader's image, credibility, or ability to inspire the team. Quite the contrary, it actually enhances it. But to do this, a leader needs a sense of self-value regardless of the outcome.

- Build trust and connect to people by purposely and strategically revealing your past failure or vulnerability.

- Take blame; ask for help; admit that you blew it. It is an opportunity to build human bonds and connection.

- Simply say, "I don't know," and point to a better source of expertise (your subordinate or peer). It is an opportunity to show your confidence and build trust not only with the person who asks you but also (enormously) with the person you refer them to, since you make them shine at your own expense.

QUESTIONS TO CONSIDER

✓ *How can you strategically reveal your plans to your competition and shape their reaction to your advantage?*

✓ *How can you build trust in your team or organization by giving someone else the glory?*

✓ *How do you motivate your team by revealing yourself and getting them involved?*

Stratagem 33:
The Double-Agent Ploy

*When the enemy lays traps, set a trap within his traps
to create internal discord. Use the enemy's spies to
spy for you, and you will not lose the battle.*

—The 36 Stratagems

LONG AGO IN CHINA

During the Three Kingdoms period (A.D. 220-591), the most
highly regarded and powerful general, named Cao Cao, was
hunting down his rival, Zhou Yu. Cao Cao's strength was fighting
on dry land since he and his men had grown up on the central
plains of China, whereas Zhou Yu had won many victories fighting
in wetland areas. Therefore, Cao Cao could never strike the final
blow against Zhou You when they fought near riverbanks or
marshes.

Cao Cao hired two generals experienced in aquatic warfare to
train and lead his men, and on whom his victory would depend.
While his men were training to swim rivers and navigate through
marshes, Cao Cao also pursued a nonviolent strategy. He ordered
one of his advisers, who was Zhou Yu's old friend, to visit Zhou
Yu and try to persuade him to surrender.

Zhou Yu welcomed his old friend with great warmth and a
lavish banquet, reliving the old times and friendship while refusing
to talk of politics and war. Zhou Yu seemed to drink a lot, and
by late that night, he looked really drunk. He told the adviser to
stay for the night. The adviser could not sleep a wink. Believing
that Zhou Yu was deep in drunken slumbers, he snooped around
and found a stack of letters on Zhou Yu's desk. He hastily went

through them to find a shocking letter from the two aquatic-warfare generals whom Cao Cao had hired. The letter said that the two were ready to form an alliance with Zhou Yu. They would soon behead Cao Cao and send his head to Zhou Yu. The letter was a forgery, of course, planted by Zhou Yu to sow distrust in Cao Cao's camp.

The next day, the adviser immediately headed back to Cao Cao's camp. Hearing the adviser's report, Cao Cao ordered the immediate execution of the two generals without giving them a chance to defend themselves. They died and, with them, Cao Cao's only chance of conquering Zhou Yu.

MODERN APPLICATIONS

Modern Industrial Espionage

These days, a Korean or Taiwanese firm can hire a retired Japanese engineer or field technician at a reasonable price. Thus, they can learn advanced technology from the Japanese really quickly. Samsung, for example, by welcoming the brightest engineers from Sony, could "borrow" the existing technology that Sony had developed. Companies can wage legitimate industrial espionage by hiring employees who have the expertise and deep knowledge of a competitor.

Google established a recruiting office in Kirkland, Washington, a five-minute drive from Microsoft headquarters, for the sole purpose of recruiting Microsoft talent. When Kai Fu Lee, head of the Interactive Services Division, left Microsoft for Google, he set off a series of lawsuits between the two companies regarding the noncompetition agreement.

Chinese, Japanese, Singaporean, and Taiwanese are best at adopting and adapting Western technology. They apply the double-agent ploy in many ways: sending their best talent to America to attend the best schools and then bringing them back home with a well-rounded exposure to the best in the world;

buying a product and tearing it apart to make something similar; or refining someone else's product to make it even better.

Using Big Data as a Spy

I have been thinking about buying a new set of furniture, so I've been looking at different models and comparing prices online. Moments after beginning my search, I receive an e-mail from Amazon.com with an offer on some particular furniture that is similar to what I have been looking for. The Amazon ad follows me to almost every site I visit, appearing on the right side of my screen. I also notice that Amazon recommends other models under "Items that you might be interested in." Has Amazon been spying on me? In a word, *yes.* How does Amazon know that I am looking for this particular model with those specific features? Despite feeling a little creepy, I am swayed by the convenience and make a purchase from Amazon.

It occurs to me that Nordstrom also spied on me when I was hunting for a particular white halter dress. Moments after I began the online search for the dress, Nordstrom relentlessly followed me, displaying specific dresses of different brands. Amazingly, they varied slightly in brand and price, yet never failed to include the three salient specs: halter cut, white, and semicasual style.

Rachel Wolfson writes on bigdatanews.com (December 11, 2013) that Nordstrom, Amazon, and many other retailers use big data—"the spy"—to see what a customer has viewed and what they have bought. This method is called "item-to-item collaborative filtering"—a technique that uses structured and unstructured data sources to tailor a returning customer's shopping experience. By analyzing the shopping history, a retailer can offer a customer exactly what she wants, through any smart device. Big data's real-time processing enables effective inventory management whereby a store can avoid being over- or understocked. It also pinpoints what merchandise to display and where, specifically, to display it for the customer's convenience.

According to Steve Lohr of the *New York Times* (February 11, 2012), in a broader sense, big data helps businesses make sense of the flood of information—social media; Web traffic; and digital sensors in industrial equipment, automobiles, electrical meters, and shipping crates—to guide decisions. Retailers such as Walmart analyze sales; pricing; and economic, demographic, and weather data to tailor product selections at particular stores and determine what items to mark down and when. Shipping companies such as UPS leverage data on truck delivery times and traffic patterns to calibrate logistics. Nordstrom combines using big data, following on social media, and recording both online and brick-and-mortar purchases to determine shopping behavior, patterns, and trends. Online dating services such as Match.com sort through their data of personal characteristics, and interactions of their members to improve the algorithms for matching up dates.

Using Big Data—for now, anyway—is a serious investment. But it gives a new competitive advantage, and the payoff is already significant. Professor Erik Brynjolfsson, an economist at MIT's Sloan School of Management, says business decisions will increasingly be based on data and analysis rather than on experience and intuition. "We can start being a lot more scientific," he observes.

IMPLEMENTATION TACTICS

What enables the wise sovereign and the general to strike and conquer and to achieve things beyond the reach of ordinary men is foreknowledge. Now, this foreknowledge cannot be elicited from spirits; it cannot be obtained inductively from experience, nor by any deductive calculation. Knowledge of the enemy's dispositions can be obtained only from other men. Hence, there are five types of agents that can be used: local agents, inside agents, double agents, doomed agents, and surviving agents.

—Sun Tzu

Kenrick Cleveland at maxpersuasion.com gives the following tips:

- *Local agent:* Find old connections, classmates, or friends who work for your opponent.

- *Inside agent:* Recruit people from your competitor. Look for those who have resentments or are demotivated, pushed aside, or under difficult circumstances.

- *Double agent:* Train and send your own agent to your competitor and have him report back.

- *Doomed agent:* Send expendable agents who plant false information.

- *Surviving agent:* Seek out agents whom your competitor has sent to spy on you. Entice him and use him.

This stratagem suggests using your competition's spy against him to create discord and confusion in the enemy camp. In war, espionage is an acceptable practice to gain vital information about your enemy's movements. In today's business, hiring the right people, recruiting your competition's key talents, using (legal) tracking technology, and purchasing vital data such as big data are legitimate modern forms of espionage.

Be subtle! And use your spies in every kind of business.

—Sun Tzu

- Headhunt key talent from your competition's talent pool.

- Use governmental agencies or officials who are in an industry where they previously had regulatory power or knowledge.

- Use agents to sow discord and conflict within your competitor's camp.

- Have the vital information and data—this is critical.

Kaihan Krippendorff comments in his book, *Hide a Dagger behind a Smile,* that we are living in a society of webs of connection and relationships. Identifying the relationship that your competition depends on generates your levers of influence. By pinpointing your competition's vital relationship and finding the best way to influence it, you create opportunities for gaining an advantage. Google did it by influencing Lee Kai Fu, a former president of Microsoft China.

QUESTIONS TO CONSIDER

✓ *What vital relationship does your competition rely on, and how can you topple or penetrate it?*

✓ *What information do you need to have in order to gain an advantage?*

✓ *How do you resort to your web of connections and leverage it for inside information?*

Stratagem 34:
The Self-Injury Scheme

People seldom inflict injuries on themselves intentionally, so when someone gets hurt, it is perceived as real. Exploit this naïveté to gain your enemy's trust, thus sowing discord among his troops. This is how you trick him, just as if he were a babe in the woods.

—The 36 Stratagems

Long Ago in China

During the Spring and Autumn period, He Lu killed the emperor of Wu and declared himself emperor. The deceased emperor's son, Qing Li, was gathering brave and able men to overthrow He Lu. Fearing the intelligent and brave prince Qing Li, He Lu hired Yao Li to assassinate the prince.

Yao Li was physically tiny but brave and smart. He revealed to He Lu his drastic scheme to assassinate Qing Li. First, Yao Li was arrested for publicly offending the emperor. To make the arrest more credible, his right arm was chopped off. He later was secretly released, but the emperor announced that he had escaped from prison, and had his entire family executed.

Yao Li then sought refuge at the prince's camp and swore loudly to seek revenge. Upon seeing the stump of his amputated arm and hearing the story about his family, Qing Li trusted him and kept him as his assistant. Yao Li was sailing on the same boat with Qing Li. When the boat was in the middle of the sea, Yao Li took out a spear and thrust it into Qing Li. As the prince bled to death, his men captured Yao Li. When they came near the border, Yao Li committed suicide with a sword.

MODERN APPLICATIONS

Nordstrom Injures Itself to Retain Its Customer-Centric Values

In December 2012, my uncle-in-law, while flying from Montgomery, Alabama, to Chicago for a wedding, unfortunately lost his luggage when changing planes in Atlanta. After a phone call, a Nordstrom sales representative delivered to his hotel room a few outfits for him to choose for the morning service and the wedding reception. For many decades, Nordstrom's customer-centric culture has been well known and widely admired as the gold standard in the U.S. retail industry. Nordstrom is famous for the brevity of its employee handbook:

Nordstrom Rules: Rule #1: Use your good judgment in all situations. There will be no additional rules. Please feel free to ask your department manager, store manager, or division general manager any question at any time.

Frontline employees are empowered to make decisions. These can be as creative as handwriting a thank-you note or personally delivering merchandise to a customer's location.

Nordstrom is best known for its liberal return policy. Customers are free to return their unwanted Nordstrom purchases back to the store with no time limit and may even receive full-price cash refunds, no matter how much time has elapsed. According to Cotten Timberlake, Renee Dudley, and Chris Burritt in *Bloomberg Businessnewsweek* (October 2013), many retailers have long lived by the philosophy that the customer is king, and have adopted liberal return policies in the hopes of winning the loyalty of free-spending shoppers. But the recent economic downturn, combined with increasing return fraud, has moved many retailers to take a stronger stand in fighting the industry's $8.8-billion-a-year return fraud. Such fraud includes returning stolen merchandise or merchandise purchased with fraudulent tender, collusion, return of used merchandise, and counterfeit receipts. While many retailers, including Macy's, Bloomingdales,

T.J. Maxx, and REI, tighten their return policies and use different approaches to prevent loss, Nordstrom stands firm in its policy. "Our experience is that if you treat the customer with respect, they respect you back," says Colin Johnson, a spokesman for Nordstrom.

To adapt to increasingly price-conscious customers, Nordstrom has adjusted its merchandise mix to include lower-priced items and lower-priced versions of existing designer apparel lines. The average selling price of merchandise in Nordstrom stores was reportedly about 10 percent lower in 2009 than in 2008. Nordstrom's pricing rollback efforts hurt its sales revenues in 2008 and 2009, but 2009 same-store sales comparisons show that it made steady improvement. To further its expansion, the company launched a multichannel platform that gives e-commerce customers a "buy online, in-store pickup" option. And to serve global customers, it has made its online shopping available in thirty additional countries. To make it more accessible, Nordstrom Rack stores, which carry past-season and lower-priced merchandise, are rolling out to strip malls in addition to opening in regular stores.

Nordstrom has inflicted the "self-injury" stratagem in many ways to maintain an unwavering commitment to its customer-centric values. This includes giving employees total autonomy to conduct a business as an entrepreneur, offering the most liberal return policies, rolling back prices, offering a greater merchandise mix, and extending local and global reach at different price points and geography. Its financial performance, even in recession, has proved that "self-injury" to retain a customer relationship is a sound strategy (if you can afford it).

Self-Injury to Build Client Base and Expand Market Share

Jeff Bezos, CEO of Amazon, is the ultimate believer in using the self-injury stratagem to expand market share. All Amazon businesses are at razor-thin margins, sometimes even at "nonprofit" status. Amazon sells ultracheap database software for businesses, losing dollars on the bet that it can earn them back somewhere else or in the long term. For example, membership in Amazon Prime provides free two-day shipping on all orders, free streaming of online movies and TV shows, and one free Kindle book to borrow monthly—all for seventy-nine dollars a year. It is estimated, however, that Amazon spends an average of more than ninety dollars annually per customer to supply Prime's services. That's a net loss of at least eleven dollars per customer, adding up to hundreds of millions in annual losses for Amazon. Why does Amazon keep this money-losing service? It's part of the grand "self-injury" scheme to win customers' loyalty for a lifetime. As a Prime member myself, I go to Amazon to buy everything from books to birthday gifts, to Israeli couscous. Amazon Prime makes it too dangerously convenient for me to switch to other retailers: discounted price, two-day delivery, and one-click checkout.

At the early stages, Alibaba successfully practiced "self-injury" by offering free listings to vendors to lure them from Ebay China to its auction site. Lenovo declared "a summer of massacre" in 2004. It tried to take out powerful rivals such as Dell, Hewlett Packer, and Toshiba, as well as local rivals, by launching a huge promotion with over a hundred kinds of products. Meanwhile, the company's board of directors "injured itself" by slashing the compensation for its members by an average of 40 percent and lowering CEO Yang Yuanqing's pay by half. Business revived and set a new high record—something the company had not managed to do in over two years before the "self-injury" strategy.

"Happy hour," "ladies' night," "Tuesdays free," "dollar item," "buy one, get one free"—all these are self-injury tactics to lure customers to your site or build up sales volume.

Beware of using this stratagem unless you are well capitalized and have a solid strategic plan. It could backfire. Lots of mom-and-pop restaurants in Atlanta and New York City go bankrupt in the first six months when, after a month of heavy discounts and free food, the customers don't keep coming back when the promotion is over.

Groupon and Scoutmob use the "self-injury" stratagem heavily.

Individual vendors such as massage therapists, local restaurants, hair salons, and flower services sign up and agree to heavy discounts of up to 70 percent—and often suffer the same fate as those restaurants. My massage therapist was exploited by clever customers who used many heavily discounted coupons and never returned when the full price went into effect. While "self-injury" could work as a means to build a client base, it can also destroy a small business that injures itself too deeply without enough financial backup. Many people exploit these Groupon and Scoutmob incentives and never become regular customers.

IMPLEMENTATION TACTICS

In the book *The 36 Strategies of the Chinese,* Wee Chow Hou and Lan Luh Luh suggest that this stratagem is typically used to gain market share or client base quickly, to remain in the market till the situation shifts in the business's favor, to overcome short-term difficulties, to stimulate demand and counter competition. It can also be used to cut losses when getting crumbs is still better than having no bread at all. Make sure you are financially strong enough to weather the injury you inflict on yourself.

- Offer a heavy discount to attract customers and promote sales.

- Lower the price to gain market share; then raise the price to make profit later.

- Use different marketing schemes to lure customers to your site and get them hooked.

- Don't go into a "self-injury" scheme without a viable plan and the financial wherewithal to weather the loss.

This also suggests that people tend to disregard the weak, and hesitate to cause them further pain. When you pose no threat and are discounted by your competition, you benefit from reserving your strength and resources to build your own power within this protective bubble.

- Hide your strength to appear less intimidating so that you can get your foot in the door.

- Use this self-deprecation to feign weakness or create a pleasant, noncompetitive atmosphere while awaiting the right moment to strike.

QUESTIONS TO CONSIDER

✓ *What is your objective now: expand market share or make a profit?*

✓ *How do you mobilize your resources to serve your objective?*

✓ *How do you "injure yourself" to gain an advantage?*

✓ *How could you appear less threatening in order to get what you want?*

Stratagem 35:
Linking Stratagem

If the enemy has a powerful army, do not attack head-on. Instead, use a combination of different stratagems to weaken his power. Good leadership and clever plots play a critical role in winning a battle, as if a clever commander had heaven's blessings.

—The 36 Stratagems

LONG AGO IN CHINA

The prince of Chu was held prisoner by the state of Qi. The state of Qi would release the prince on the condition that he give up the eastern part of his territory. After returning home, the new king of Chu was reluctant to keep his promise. He asked his three best generals to give him advice. The first advised him to deliver on his promise, or else his reputation and authority would be jeopardized. The second adviser said the eastern territory was too big to give up, and offered to lead his troops to defend the eastern border. The third general agreed with the second one but added that they should form an alliance with a large neighboring state for reinforcement.

The new king of Chu thought about his options and decided to pursue them all. The next day, he told the first general to send the state of Qi a message that he would surrender the eastern territory as agreed. Then, on the second day, he told the second general to follow his own advice and lead the troops to the eastern border, prepared to defend against any attack from Qi. On the third day, he told the third general to lead a diplomatic mission to neighboring Qin to request alliance and reinforcement.

Confused and furious at the different messages they were receiving from Chu's actions, the Qi decided to launch an attack and take Chu's eastern land by force. When Qi's reinforcements arrived and lined up to start a head-on battle against Chu's, the third general arrived, escorted by the Qin troops. Furthermore, Qin's army was led by a renowned Qin general who was ready to join forces with Chu. Outnumbered, the king of Qi called off the onslaught, leaving Chu's eastern lands intact.

MODERN APPLICATIONS

Alibaba Thwarts Ebay China

In 1999, Jack Ma, a Chinese teacher of the English language, started Alibaba.com as a business-to-business portal connecting small Chinese manufacturers with buyers overseas. In 2002, Ebay entered China with a grand plan to dominate the online auction market, as it had done in America. Ebay China acquired Eachnet for $180 million and became Ebay Eachnet to give itself a local presence in China. According to Helen H. Wang's book *The Chinese Dream,* after the acquisition, Ebay hired a German manager to run the China operation and brought in a chief technology officer from the United States. Neither of them spoke Chinese or understood the local business culture. (What was Ebay corporate management thinking?) The operations were then moved to California, which made for slow decision making and stalled transmission speed. For example, it could take *nine months* to change one line of text on the Web site. The whole operation system was a textbook example of the stratagem "Lure the tiger from its mountain lair." Here on foreign turf, Ebay lacked the strength it had when operating in its home country.

That same year, Jack Ma took on Ebay in China by launching a competing consumer-to-consumer auction site called Taobao ("find treasure"). He did it not to make money but to fend off EBay from taking away Alibaba's customers. Many industry observers criticize the sustainability of Alibaba's "self-injury" strategy, which Jack Ma at first used to lure customers away from Ebay Eachnet to his site Taobao. To "trap" them there, Taobao made its Web site highly customer- and product-centric, with many categories and user-friendly features that Ebay Eachnet did not provide, thanks to Taobao's deep understanding of its Chinese market and business culture.

The unavailability of a payment system had created tremendous barriers in the growth of e-commerce in China. Like the Vietnamese, most Chinese did not possess credit cards. Business was transacted using cash or bank wire transfers. Because of the strict regulations for foreign banks, Ebay was not fast enough to introduce the Paypal payment system to China. Meanwhile, Jack Ma, comprehending Chinese payment habits and preferences, "stole a goat along the way" by seizing the opportunity to launch Alipay—an escrow service that consumers can use to verify that they are happy with goods they have bought, before releasing money to the seller. Ma offered this service to protect buyers left vulnerable by China's notoriously weak consumer protection laws. Alipay became the driving force for Taobao's exponential growth. Launching Alipay "pulled the firewood" from under Ebay China's "pot" by nullifying the Paypal payment system, Ebay's core competency. It also "shut the doors to trap the thief"—the customers on Taobao and Alibaba, using its Alipay payment system, which completes the encircling trap of customer convenience: the one-stop shop.

Gaining momentum, Ma focused advertising on major television channels, where he believes the less sophisticated masses in China spend their time rather than on the Internet. (Ebay wrongly did the opposite.) In 2005, Taobao's market share jumped to 59 percent; in March 2006, it reached 67 percent; in August 2007, it hit 83 percent. In late 2006, the Ebay Eachnet site was shut down. Meg Whitman, CEO of Ebay, announced a new joint venture with billionaire Li Ka Shing's Chinese portal TOM Online, which provides wireless value-added multimedia service. The partnership is also Ebay's formal farewell to the online auction market in China.

Alibaba's thwarting of Ebay China was a masterful use of multiple linking stratagems.

Diapers.com: Fighting the Behemoth Amazon

Amazon, one of the most competitive and successful companies on the planet, maintains its advantage not by executing one strategy, not by relying on its superior competitive edge, but by constantly implementing different "linking strategies" to knock down its competition.

Brad Stone writes in his book *The Everything Store: Jeff Bezos and the Age of Amazon* that Amazon has a secretive group called Competitive Intelligence—its "spy" team. The team buys large volumes of merchandise from other online retailers, measuring the speed, quality, and convenience of their services. Its job is to investigate whether any rival is outperforming Amazon. The team then presents the data to the senior team, which addresses the emerging threat and finds solutions to catch up fast.

In the late 2000s, the "spy" team began tracking a rival named Quidsi, a start-up under the Web site Diapers.com, which sells diapers, baby wipes, infant formula, clothes, strollers, and other vital supplies for new parents. In 2009, Amazon offered to buy the start-up, but owners Lore and Bhara turned it down, saying they wanted to keep the company private. Soon after, Quidsi noticed Amazon dropping prices up to 30 percent on diapers and other baby products. At first, Quidsi fixed its prices and then watched as Amazon's Web site changed its prices accordingly. Amazon uses pricing bots—"spy" software that monitors other companies' prices—and adjusts Amazon's prices to match.

At first, Diapers.com could weather Amazon's attack, thanks to its strong brand and word of mouth among young parents. The company had grown from nothing to $300 million in annual sales in only a few years. But it could not continue to hold its ground when the giant Amazon continued to slash prices—"injure itself"—and zero in on the category. Diapers.com's sales started to stagnate, and venture capitalists were reluctant to pump in additional capital. For the first time, Lore and Bhara wavered.

Meanwhile, Walmart was trying to beef up its online division. To make up ground lost to Amazon, Walmart.com offered to buy Diapers.com at around $450 million. In September 2010, Lore and Bhara traveled to Amazon's headquarters in Seattle to discuss the possibility of Amazon's acquiring Diapers.com. While they were in the meeting, Amazon sent a press release to launch a service called Amazon Mom. The service would provide a year's worth of free two-day shipping and an additional 30 percent off the already discounted diapers if the customer signed up for a service called Subscribe and Save. Not only did Amazon "beat the grass to startle the snake," but its Subscribe and Save served as a "trap" to lure customers from Diapers.com to Amazon Mom. Amazon was willing to lose $100 million over three months—that is, "injure itself" again in the diaper category, to compete with Diapers.com and "take the firewood" from under Diapers.com's "pot."

In the end, Amazon offered Quidsi $540 million and gave its owners 48 hours to respond, making clear that the Amazon Mom assault would continue if the acquisition did not come through. By the time Walmart counterbid Amazon and jacked up the price to $600 million, Quidsi had tentatively accepted Amazon's terms. Quidsi planned to let the Amazon deal expire, and then resume negotiations with Walmart. But Amazon's pressure and its willingness to drive the diaper price down to zero intimidated Quidsi, and Lore and Bhara announced the company's sale to Amazon on November 8, 2010.

IMPLEMENTATION TACTICS

Using a combination of different stratagems allows more flexibility. If one stratagem fails, another is in place to back the play. Also, combining generates new stratagems. Interlocking stratagems makes it a complex and hard-to-predict scheme, so you can apply several stratagems at once or in succession to achieve your goal. Successful companies such as Hyundai, Samsung, Apple, Walmart, Alibaba, and Amazon all use linking stratagems. Remember:

- Never rely on one stratagem for success, lest your competitor counter or replicate it.

- Use linking stratagems to generate new ones.

- Use interlocking stratagems to create an unpredictable strategy.

QUESTIONS TO CONSIDER

✓ *What stratagems fit your situation?*

✓ *How can you combine them to create an unpredictable new stratagem?*

✓ *What possibilities emerge when you combine the stratagems?*

Stratagem 36:
The Escape Ploy

Avoid engaging an obviously stronger enemy. Retreat and wait for the right moment to advance again. According to military principles, it is best to avoid confronting a stronger enemy when you are in a desperate situation.

—The 36 Stratagems

LONG AGO IN CHINA

During the Spring and Autumn period, the state of Chu was surrounded by many smaller neighboring states, which paid tribute to the emperor of Chu. But during the reign of Chu Zhuang Wang, when Chu suffered from famine, the neighboring small states attacked it.

The emperor of Chu sent small detachments of troops to defend his state instead of summoning the main army, for fear that a stronger army might ambush them and Chu would lose everything.

In one battle against the army of Yong, General Ji Li led his men and quickly invaded the Yong's territory. But the people of Yong defended their state fiercely, and it was impossible for the Chu army to take them down. Instead of summoning a big army to take Yong by brute force, General Ji Li ordered his men to retreat and feign defeat by the Yong army. He even commanded his troops to lose seven successive battles against the Yong. The Yong army grew arrogant and assumed that it would be able to defeat the Chu army with little effort. Meanwhile, the emperor of Chu led reinforcements to join with General Ji Li's troops and launch a massive attack on the Yong army. Unprepared for the massive surprise attack, The state of Yong fell to the Chu army.

MODERN APPLICATIONS:

> *Retreat is another form of advance. A*
> *smart man does not fight a losing battle.*
>
> —Chinese proverb

The An Nam Group Rejects the False Glitter of Gold

Like many Saigonese as well as international tourists, I love the upscale An Nam Group of restaurants, owned by Mr. Ly and his family. The differentiation that makes the restaurants succeed is the sophistication in food preparation, together with the charming, unforgettable ambience they create for diners. In the bloom of success, Mr. Ly bought a popular English pub in the heart of Saigon. The pub featuring top musicians, jam-packed every night with locals as well as tourists and expats, was the talk of Saigon connoisseurs. In my interview, Mr. Ly confided that the glamour and glitz had completely distracted him from focusing on the bottom line. The exorbitant rent and the top fees for well-known musicians gobbled up his profits, and the space had no capacity to expand and add more customers. After a year running the pub, Ly painfully realized that not all that glitters is gold. No matter how crowded the place got every night, every month he paid out of his pocket, unable to break even after overpaying for everything to sustain the same ambience. It was time to end the attachment—a task he found just as heartbreaking as ending a love affair.

Walmart's Bumpy Global Expansion

According to Anil K. Gupta, Vijay Govindarajan, and Haiyan Wang in their book *The Quest for Global Dominance,* Walmart's global expansion came at the price of some expensive lessons learned. The company abruptly withdrew from Hong Kong and Indonesia after learning the hard way about managing operations separated by immense differences in geography, time zones, cultures, and politics. Walmart also left the South Korean market in 2006, selling its sixteen stores for $882 million to Shinsegae Company and incurring a pretax gain of $103 million. In the same year, Walmart sold its stores in Germany to Metro for a $1 billion loss. In 2006, Walmart's gross sales in China, with a presence in thirty-six cities, reached $1.4 billion. Like many companies, Walmart adopted the strategy of penetrating a single large market and expanding the size there rather than entering many smaller markets. For example, achieving 5 percent of a market such as China would be better than a 30 percent market share in all the smaller markets of Vietnam, Laos, Cambodia, Myanmar, and Thailand combined.

Some American and European pharmaceutical companies choose to withdraw from certain developing countries due to corruption and bad practices. Staying longer not only would damage their brand and credibility, but it may also lose them their license back home.

Bank of America withdrew from Vietnam in 1997 for similar reasons. It was unfamiliar with the culture and spending and borrowing habits, and stifled by the lack of regulation in the banking and financial sector.

Best Buy closed many stores in China. It was losing money because the haggling, frugal Chinese would come to Best Buy to check the prices, then buy cheaper brands next door.

KFC withdrew from Hong Kong in 1967, then come back strong. Its presence all over Asia is very unlike its "cheap fast food" image in the United States. In Asia, it is positioned as a modern lifestyle choice for the up-and-coming middle class. Beside capitalizing on the social and demographic trend, KFC learned to use Hong Kong and Taiwanese managers, who understand both East and West, as executives and managers of KFC in China. (In the past, American managers who were hopelessly unfamiliar with Chinese culture were diagnosed as a big part of KFC's failure in the pioneer days).

Recently, L'Oreal pulled its Garnier skin-care brand out of

China, a week after Revlon withdrew altogether from the Chinese market. Complex distribution channels and aggressive local online sellers made them unable to compete effectively. Unlike other high-end cosmetic brands, L'Oreal and Revlon had no competitive advantage, and competing solely on price made their business model unsustainable in a cutthroat Chinese market.

Panasonic Escapes

Bruce Einhorn, Mariko Yasu, and Takashi Amano write in *Bloomberg Businessweek* (February 13, 2014) that many Japanese consumer electronics giants, in trying to be all things to all people, making everything from cameras and smart phones to solar panels, have suffered tough losses. Sony, fighting domestic rivals while facing fierce competition from lower-cost manufacturers in China (Lenovo, Huawei) and Korea (SamSung, LG), has announced that it expects to lose $1.1 billion in the fiscal year ending March 2014. Panasonic lost a combined 1.5 trillion yen ($14.6 billion) in the two years ending in March 2013. Panasonic CEO Kazuhiro Tsuga realized it was high time to use the escape ploy, to get the company out of money-losing businesses and focus on new ventures. Tsuga has suspended production of panels for plasma TVs and cut back on circuit board manufacturing, is selling semiconductor assembly plants in Asia, and is quitting developing smartphones altogether. The key is to avoid fighting head-on with stronger rivals Samsung and Apple and hemorrhaging money in the process. Instead, it has started to build relationships with electric car makers such as Tesla Motors, which has agreed to buy two billion battery cells from Panasonic over four years. In addition to batteries, Panasonic is focusing on auto safety devices such as 360-degree-view cameras.

The strategy is beginning to pay off after its restructuring, using the "escape ploy" to jettison unprofitable businesses." Operating profits from batteries for electric cars jumped to 28.2 billion yen ($275 million) in the last quarter of 2013, compared with a loss of 800 million yen ($7.8 million) the year before. Profits for the company as a whole increased 20 percent in the quarter. Rating experts wrote,

"Panasonic made earlier decisions than Sony to exit unprofitable businesses. The result is a slimmer and nimbler organization that gives Panasonic the opportunity to continue its recovery."

IMPLEMENTATION TACTICS

When faced with certain defeat, one has three options: surrender, negotiate for peace, and retreat. Surrendering implies total defeat. Negotiating for peace implies partial defeat. But escape does not imply defeat. By running away, one can preserve strength and keep alive the possibility of launching an attack later, at the right place or with the right timing. Withdrawing from an industry or market where you are no longer competitive is a smart move. Panasonic has proved that. Remember, just as in war, business's fate is not necessarily determined by a single battle.

- Choose your battle wisely.
- Choose or predict the timing and battlefield (place).
- Retreat one step to progress three steps.
- Be decisive in cutting your losses.
- Be aware of emotional attachments that could get in the way of your cutting loose.
- Never fall in love with a deal.

QUESTIONS TO CONSIDER

✓ *What area/product/market should you escape from?*

✓ *What will be the impacts and ramifications of your retreat or escape?*

✓ *What resources could the escape free up, and how do you make use of them to gain an advantage?*

Acknowledgments

I could never have completed this book without the encouragement of my family, friends, and colleagues, who have been my bedrock of support.

To my mother, Phuong, who has been a role model and inspiration, thanks for being my number one heroine.

To my sister, Ivy, who has always been there for me, thanks for being who you are to keep me in balance.

To my husband, Doug, and my sons, Joshua and Levi, who have been a tremendous source of inspiration, encouragement, and material, thank you for your love, support, and patience.

To my friend and Chinese-language teacher Jue Li, thank you for keeping my interpretation of the Chinese text on target.

To my editor, Michael Carr, who worked side by side with me, thanks for bringing the best out of me.

To my colleague and mentor Jim Dawson, who has been guiding my efforts in writing this book and in my career, thank you for your friendship, collegiality, and wisdom throughout the years.

I owe special thanks to the following friends and colleagues, who helped guide my efforts in writing this book: Jack Perry, Rich St. Dennis, Jennifer Kahnweiler, Ken Futch, Kelly Vandever, Tom Nixon, Judy Rogers, Dawn Bui, Nguyen Thanh Huong, Natalie Nguyen, Jessica Lu, and Mike Wien.

I have been immensely lucky to have the support of these and many other people too numerous to mention here. I am indebted to all of you who helped along the way in the production of this book.

About the Author

Lan Bercu is the founder and president of Lead Across Cultures International, an Atlanta, Georgia, based company with a focus on cross-cultural competence and global leadership. As an international speaker and expert in her field, Lan has nearly two decades of experience working with international corporations in Asia and North America, among them Intel, Bayer, and Morgan Stanley Smith Barney.

Born and raised in Vietnam, as a young girl Lan was inspired by the Chinese classics The Thirty-Six Chinese Stratagems and Sun Tzu's The Art of War. The principals, tactics, and strategies in the books helped her overcome the tremendous hardships she and her family faced during and after the Vietnam War. These messages carried her through, enabling her not only to survive but also to thrive in academia as well as on corporate battlefields and in entrepreneurial rivalries.

Lan received her MBA from Kennesaw State University. She is past president of the Toastmasters Club of the Metro Atlanta Chamber of Commerce and is a member of the National Speakers Association and the Global Speakers Federation. Lan has frequently been featured in Entrepreneur magazine and on Finance Business News Channel, Vietnam Investment Review, and other media channels.

CONTACT:

LeadAcrossCultures.com

Lan@LeadAcrossCultures.com

Tel: 404-512-9909 (USA)

Working with the Author

Lan Bercu is an international speaker and expert on cross-cultural competence and global leadership. She is well known for her content-rich, high-energy, interactive presentations that provide tools the audience can use right now.

KEYNOTE PRESENTATIONS, SEMINARS AND WORKSHOPS

The programs run from twenty-five minutes to two days and can be customized in variety of ways including the level of interactivity and specific issues and challenges your audience is facing.

TOPICS:

Succeeding in an Intercultural Organization
- Apply global leadership techniques for fostering intercultural collaboration.
- Implement tools to improve your cross-cultural communications.
- Handle disagreements with people whose conflict resolution styles are different from yours.
- Establish positive multicultural and global relationships for bottom-line results.

The 36 Ancient Chinese Strategies for Modern Business
- Discover unconventional strategies and tactics, and adapt them for your business success.
- Implement specific strategies to free your thinking and gain the competitive edge.
- Stretch your current thinking to find new solutions to complex, fast-breaking situations.

Sun Tzu's Art of War for Professional Women
- Discover the five critical elements for your success.
- Understand the inevitable forces gathering to make the twenty-first century the women's leadership century and improve your timing to your fullest advantage.
- Transform your weak points into possibilities and conquer, even from an inferior position.

Bibliography

Adelstein, Jake, and Nathalie-Kyoko Stucky. "The Ghosts of Sony." Japan Subculture Research Center, November 13, 2012. www.japansubculture.com/the-ghosts-of-sony/.

Berfield, Susan. "Dirty Honey." *Bloomberg Businessweek,* September 19, 2013.

Berfield, Susan, and Manuel Baigorri. "Knitting a Supply Chain." *Bloomberg Businessweek,* January 2, 2014.

Bostic, Kevin. "New Samsung Ad Knocks iPhone Language Limitations, Features Goats." Apple Insider, July 5, 2013. www. Appleinsider.com.

Brogan, Chris, and K. Shelby Skrhak. "What Reality TV Stars Can Teach Us about Marketing and Branding." *Success,* February 2012.

Chu, Jing Ning. *The Asian Mind Game.* New York: Scribner's, 1991.

Christensen, Clayton. *The Innovator's Dilemma.* Boston: Harvard Business School Press, 1997.

Duhigg, Charles, and David Kocieniewski. "How Apple Sidesteps Billions in Taxes." *New York Times,* April 28, 2012.

Ebhardt, Tommaso. "An Entry-Level Maserati Woos Drivers Bored with BMW." *Bloomberg Businessweek,* July 3, 2013.

Einhorn, Bruce. "Lenovo Takes On Apple and Samsung in Smartphone Market." *Bloomberg Businessweek,* January 30, 2014.

Einhorn, Bruce, and Siddharth Philip. "An Indian Tractor Maker Tries to Run Like a Deere." *Bloomberg Businessweek,* August 6, 2013.

Eihorn, Bruce, Mariko Yasu, and Takashi Amano. "Panasonic Revives as Other Japanese Tech Giants Falter." *Bloomberg Businessweek,* February 13, 2014.

Fannin, Rebecca A. *Silicon Dragons*. New York: McGraw-Hill, 2008.

Farnham, Alan, and Susanna Kim. "Blackjack Player Who Won $15 Million From 3 Casinos Reveals How." *ABC News,* March 21, 2012.

Gallo, Carmine. "How Hyundai's New CEO Taught Me to Create an Irresistible Brand Story." *Forbes,* December 30, 2013.

Goudreau, Jenna. "Lynn Tilton: The Wild Woman of Wall Street." *Forbes,* April 7, 2011.

Gupta, Anil K., Vijay Govindarajan, and Haiyan Wang. *The Quest for Global Dominance*. New York: Wiley, 2008.

John Ellett. 3 Reasons Samsung's Latest Advertising Poking Apple Is So Smart. *Forbes,* September 20, 2012.

Krippendorff, Kaihan. *Hide a Dagger behind a Smile*. New York: Adams Media, 2008.

Lao Tzu. *Tao Te Ching*. Translated by Stephen Mitchell. New York: Harper Collins, 1988.

Lee Kuan Yew. *From Third World to First*. New York: Harper Collins, 2000.

Lev-Ram, Michal. "Samsung's Road to Mobile Domination." *Fortune,* February 2013.

Levy, Steven. *In the Plex: How Google Thinks, Works and Shapes Our Lives.* New York: Simon and Schuster, 2011.

Ling Zhi Jun. *The Lenovo Affair*. Singapore: Wiley, 2006.

Lohr, Steve. "The Age of Big Data." *New York Times,* February 11, 2012.

Ly Quy Trung. *Bau Troi Khong Chi co Mau Xanh*. Ho Chi Minh City. Tre Publishing House, 2011.

MacMillan, Douglas. "At ModCloth, Vintage Fashion Goes Mobile." *Bloomberg Businessweek,* August 8, 2013.

Minter, Adam. "To a Chinese Scrap-Metal Hunter, America's Trash Is Treasure." *Bloomberg Businessweek,* August 29, 2013.

Pressler, Jessica. "What Does It Take for a Female Tycoon to Get Noticed around Here?" *New York,* April 10, 2011.

Roberts, Dexter, and Carol Matlack. "China Turns the Screws on Multinationals." *Bloomberg Businessweek,* September 19, 2013.

Ron Kaufman. *Uplifting Service.* Ashland, OH: Evolve, 2012.

Rosenblatt, Joel. "Herbalife Wins Dismissal of Belgian 'Pyramid Scheme' Suit." *Bloomberg Businessweek,* December 6, 2013.

Sea-Jin Chang. *Sony vs Samsung: The Inside Story of the Electronics Giants' Battle for Global Supremacy.* Singapore: Wiley, 2008.

Steers, Richard M. *Made in Korea.* New York: Routledge, 1999.

Stone, Brad. "Can Marissa Mayer Save Yahoo?" *Bloomberg Businessweek,* August 6, 2013.

Stone, Brad. *The Everything Store: Jeff Bezos and the Age of Amazon.* New York: Little, Brown, 2013.

Stone, Brad, and Sarah Frier. "Facebook's Next Decade." *Bloomberg Businessweek,* February 3, 2014.

Straker, David. The Columbo Technique. *Changingminds.org*

Stross, Randall. *Planet Google.* New York: Free Press, 2008.

Sun Tzu. *Sun Tzu on the Art of War: The Oldest Treatise in the World.* Translated by Lionel Giles. Norwood, Australia: Deodand, 2002.

Timberlake, Cotten, Renee Dudley, and Chris Burritt. "Don't Even Think about Returning This Dress." *Bloomberg Businessweek,* September 26, 2013.

Touryalai, Halah. "Marriott's New Host." *Forbes,* July 2013.

Trefis Team. "Best Buy Continues to Diversify by Selling Geek Squad Services." *Forbes,* October 10, 2012.

Vise, David A. *The Google Story: Inside the Hottest Business, Media and Technology Success of Our Time.* New York: Bantam Dell, 2005.

Vo Senger, Harro. *Stratagems*. Bern, Munich, and Vienna: Scherz Verlag, 2000.

Vo Senger, Harro. *The 36 Stratagems for Business*. Singapore: Marshall Cavendish International, 2006.

Walton, Sam. *Sam Walton: Made in America*. New York: Bantam, 1993.

Wang, Helen H. *The Chinese Dream*. Kentucky. Best Seller Press, 2010.

Wee Chow Hou. *Sun Zi Bingfa: Selected Insights and Applications*. Singapore: Pearson Prentice Hall, 2005.

Wee Chow Hou and Lan Luh Luh. *The 36 Strategies of the Chinese*. Singapore: Addison Wesley, 1998.

Wingert, Pat. "The 17-Day Diet: Dr. Phil's Family Ties to Book He Touts." *Newsweek,* April 9, 2012.

Wolfson, Rachel. "Retailers Using Big Data: The Secret behind Amazon and Nordstrom's Success." *Big Data News,* December 11, 2013. www.bigdatanews.com.

Index